# HISTORIC EPWORTH

## The Heart of the Isle of Axholme

*by*
Colin Ella

Epworth Market-Place.

'I rode to Epworth which I still love beyond most places in the world'.
*(John Wesley - Journal Saturday, 26th June, 1784)*

## RURAL PUBLICATIONS

© Rural Publications and Colin Ella, 1994

ISBN 0 9522495 2 9

Set and Designed by Print - Rite, The Willows, School Lane, Stadhampton, Oxford. OX44 7TR

Printed by Alpha Print Ltd, Crawley Mill, Witney, Oxon.

*All photographs are taken by the author except where credited.*

*All rights reserved. No part of this book may be reproduced or transmitted in any form or by any means, electronic or mechanical, including photocopying, recording or by any information storage and retrieval system without permission from the Publisher in writing.*

*Title page drawing from:*
The History and Topography of the Isle of Axholme *by W.B.Stonehouse,*1839.

Epworth from the Church Field at the turn of the Century.
*Reproduced from Epworth and its Surroundings, 1903*

*Published by*
**Rural Publications**, The Willows, School Lane, Stadhampton, Oxford, OX44 7TR.    *Telephone : 01865 400002*

# CONTENTS

|  |  |  |
|---|---|---|
|  | Acknowledgements | 5 |
|  | Preface | 5 |
| *Chapter One* | The Face of Epworth Today | 7 |
| *Chapter Two* | The Farm on the Hill | 15 |
| *Chapter Three* | The Mowbray Period | 21 |
| *Chapter Four* | Town Development and Drainage Squabbles | 29 |
| *Chapter Five* | The Wesley Family | 37 |
| *Chapter Six* | Church and Chapel | 47 |
| *Chapter Seven* | Agriculture and Enclosure | 63 |
| *Chapter Eight* | Local Affairs 1630 to 1830 | 75 |
| *Chapter Nine* | The Victorian Scene | 87 |
| *Chapter Ten* | Right Up your Street | 101 |
| *Chapter Eleven* | Reflections on the Twentieth Century | 117 |

## *List of Figures*

| | | |
|---|---|---|
| *Figure One* | The Isle of Axholme in Relation to the County of Humberside. | 4 |
| *Figure Two* | Epworth in Relation to the other Villages in the Isle of Axholme. | 6 |
| *Figure Three* | Simplified Plan of Epworth Town Centre. | 8 |
| *Figure Four* | Present Day Parishes of the Isle of Axholme. | 13 |
| *Figure Five* | Flint Discoveries in the Epworth Parish. | 16 |
| *Figure Six* | Archaeological Finds in Axholme. | 18 |
| *Figure Seven* | The position of the Vinegarth in Relation to Epworth Town. | 20 |
| *Figure Eight* | Location diagram of the Excavated Trenches within the Vinegarth. | 22 |
| *Figure Nine* | Small Finds at the Vinegarth Excavations. Epworth 1975/76. | 25 |
| *Figure Ten* | The Isle of Axholme in the Early 16th Century. | 28 |
| *Figure Eleven* | Axholme and Hatfield Chace before and after the drainage of Vermuyden. | 30 |
| *Figure Twelve* | Arelebout's Map of 1639. Division of land amongst Dutch Settlers. | 33 |
| *Figure Thirteen* | Letter from John Wesley to William Wilberforce. | 38 |
| *Figure Fourteen* | Plan of Former Baptist Chapel and Graveyard in Station Road. | 52 |
| *Figure Fifteen* | Open Field Farming - Typical Strip Arrangement. | 64 |
| *Figure Sixteen* | An Impression of Strip Farming pre- and in Victorian times. | 65 |
| *Figure Seventeen* | The Manor of Epworth 1787. | 67 |
| *Figure Eighteen* | The Dispersed Settlement Pattern of Epworth 1977. | 69 |
| *Figure Nineteen* | Enclosures Allotted to John Girdham and John Cartwright. | 70 |
| *Figure Twenty* | Epworth Parish in 1857. Simplified map from Read's *History of Axholme*. | 88 |
| *Figure Twenty One* | First Edition 25" Ordnance Survey Map of Epworth Town Centre, 1886. | 94 |

## *List of Tables*

| | | |
|---|---|---|
| *Table One* | Details of Trench Excavation at the Vinegarth, Epworth. | 23 |
| *Table Two* | The Epworth Wesley Family. | 40 |
| *Table Three* | List of Rectors at St Andrews Church, Epworth. | 48 |
| *Table Four* | List of Occupations Found in Epworth in the 1850's. | 98 |

*Figure One*
**THE ISLE OF AXHOLME IN RELATION TO THE COUNTY OF HUMBERSIDE**

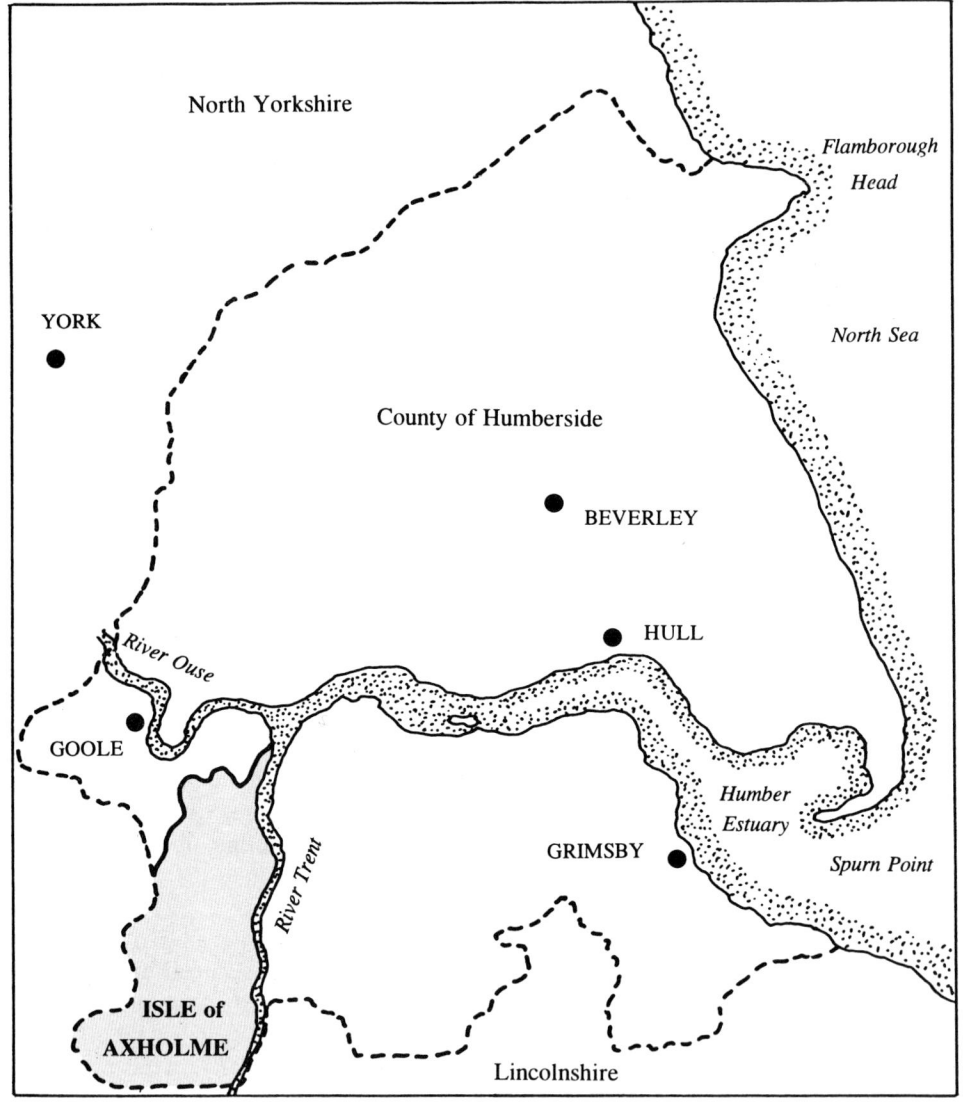

*Map not to Scale*

# Acknowledgements

I would like to express my very warm thanks to the following organisations for the time and interest shown to me in their offering of information and guidance in regard to my research. I am indebted to the Epworth Society's Information and Heritage Centre, Humberside County Council's Sites and Monuments Records in the Archaeology Unit at Beverley; the Lincolnshire Archives; the Mechanics' Institute Library, Epworth; the Public Library, Epworth, and the Scunthorpe Museum.

I also offer my special thanks to Edwin Harrison and Marjorie Trimingham for their help in supplying old photographs and also Colin Judge of Rural Publications for his encouragement and his expert and adept skill in the presentation of my efforts. I am grateful for the help of many individuals and I would like to thank the following people for their useful contributions. Bob Brewster, Ann Cooper, Vernon Cory, Margaret Fields, Peter Frost, Stephen Garner, Cliff Gravel, John Harris, Jo Harrison, Colin Hayfield, Tom Howell, Jack Stafford, Geoff Tonge, Geoff Trinder and Peter Whitehead. In addition to these I offer my thanks to people along the wayside, whose names are not known to me, but whose interesting reminiscences on Epworth's past have played a constructive part in the preparation of what follows.

*Colin Ella, 1994*

# Preface

My earlier book entitled *"Around the Isle of Axholme"*, which was published last year refers to the Isle as a little known place. Countrywide this belief holds good, but because of its associations with the Wesleys it is likely that the town of Epworth is better known than Axholme itself. Without doubt visitors regard Epworth as the Mecca of the area and its Wesleyan connections attract visitors from every corner of the world. Yet, outside the world of Methodism, Epworth is less well known, but like the whole of the Isle of Axholme, it is part of a unique district of considerable historical interest.

What follows within these pages makes no claim towards a comprehensive history, but it is hoped that it does make a reasonable attempt to unfold some of the drama and excitement of what is usually thought of as the 'capital' of the Isle of Axholme. From a brief look at the modern town, this study travels back over the centuries to examine how the very heart of Axholme has played its part in fostering the Isleonian's reputation of a sturdy independence: a dourness which has seen both gains and losses. Epworth breathes its history; the atmosphere of bygone days is ever pervasive and as much as the Wesleys are so much part of that nostalgia, the fascination of this little rural backwater extends far beyond just the influence of its most famous son.

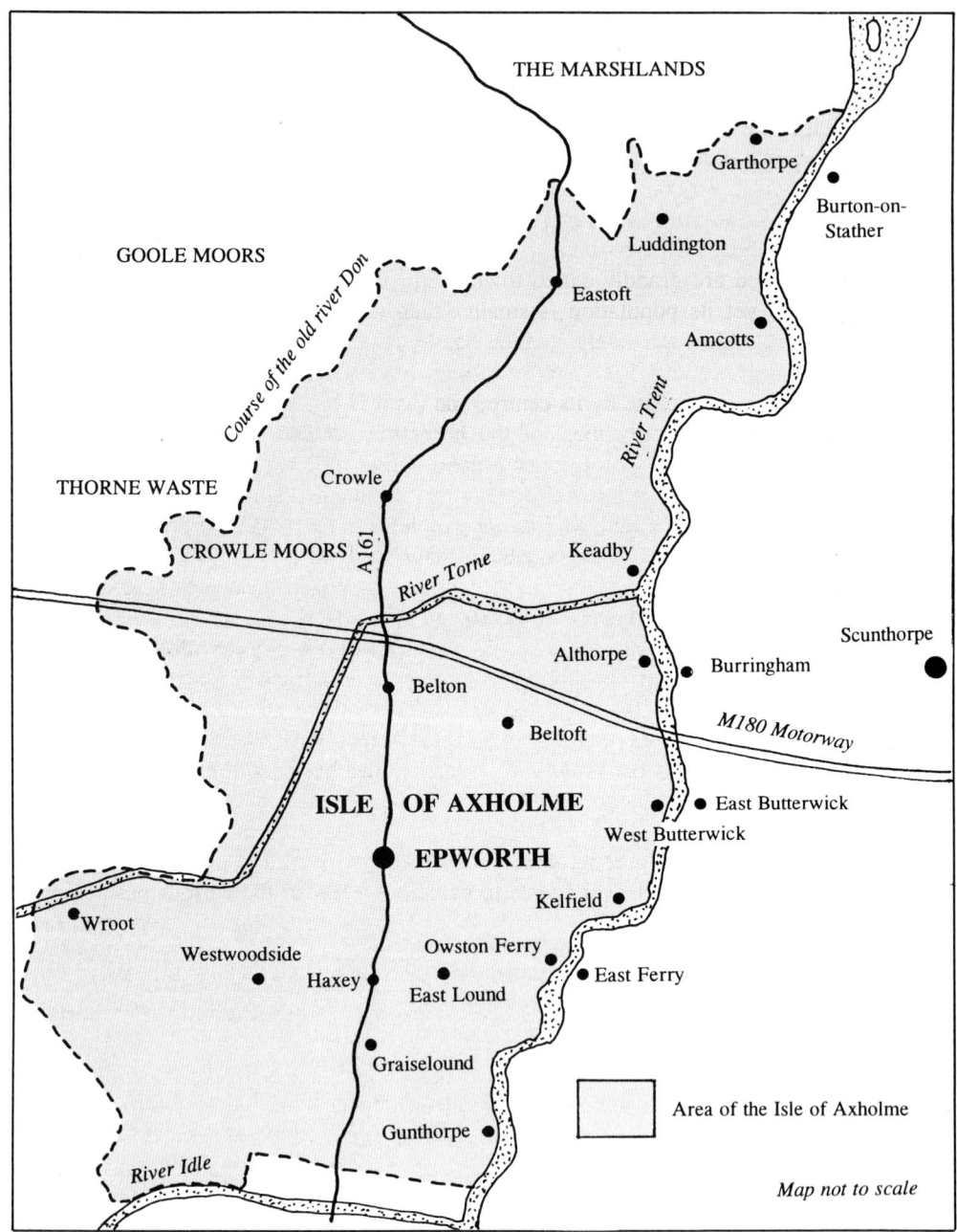

*Figure Two*
**EPWORTH IN RELATION TO THE OTHER VILLAGES IN THE ISLE OF AXHOLME**

# CHAPTER ONE

## The Face of Epworth Today

I would imagine that many people have heard of Epworth, but perhaps not the Isle of Axholme in which this popular little place is situated. Without any doubt Epworth is the busiest place in Axholme and the centre to which the vast majority of visitors make their way. The town is set in a very rural area, and 'little' is the operative word, for the whole of the Isle of Axholme has a population smaller than that of its administrative town of Goole in North Humberside.

The main centres of population are Haxey, Belton, Crowle and Epworth and the two last named are grandly called towns. Epworth is thought of as the capital of the Isle and yet its population is smaller than those of Haxey and Crowle, but with around 3400 inhabitants it does house more people than its neighbouring straggling Belton. This Mecca of Axholme has its main concentration of shops and businesses in or close by its centre, and (as it did in Victorian times) the town can again possibly supply most of the necessities of life. There are those who would like to see a revival of the erstwhile market, but it is unlikely that it could ever function in anything like its former glory. In the present economic and social framework a market might well bring problems rather than profits and would certainly complicate traffic movements through the town.

Epworth is a tourist centre mainly because of its Wesley connections and many visitors come from overseas to look at St Andrew's Church, the Wesley Memorial Church and in particular the Old Rectory which was John Wesley's boyhood home. This former Anglican Rectory is an attractive Queen Anne style house well positioned in its own grounds. There were strong objections when local planners suggested that these grounds might have been developed as a residential area and for the present at least, that idea has been shelved.

The Rectory itself dates from 1709, but the town has many other houses, barns and public buildings of considerable age. In or amongst the many listed buildings are butchers, bakers, greengrocers, supermarkets, banking facilities, building societies, estate agents, travel agents, to name but a few of the various businesses. The Holmes and Gardens Centre out along the road to Belton is a very popular venue for visitors of all ages and a fairly recent development, in a Dickensian style in Fountain's Court (off the Market Place), is another fascinating corner to visit. Here, as in the High Street, the shop fronts give reminders of the Victorian period in their window surrounds, doorways and awnings.

St Andrew's Church has overlooked the town for centuries; a symbol of Epworth's sturdy resilience and independence through the ages, from Norman times to the struggles of the 17th Century Drainage period and beyond. To stroll up Church Walk is an experience that quickly rolls back the centuries and in the peaceful tranquillity of the churchyard it is easy to recapture the days of the

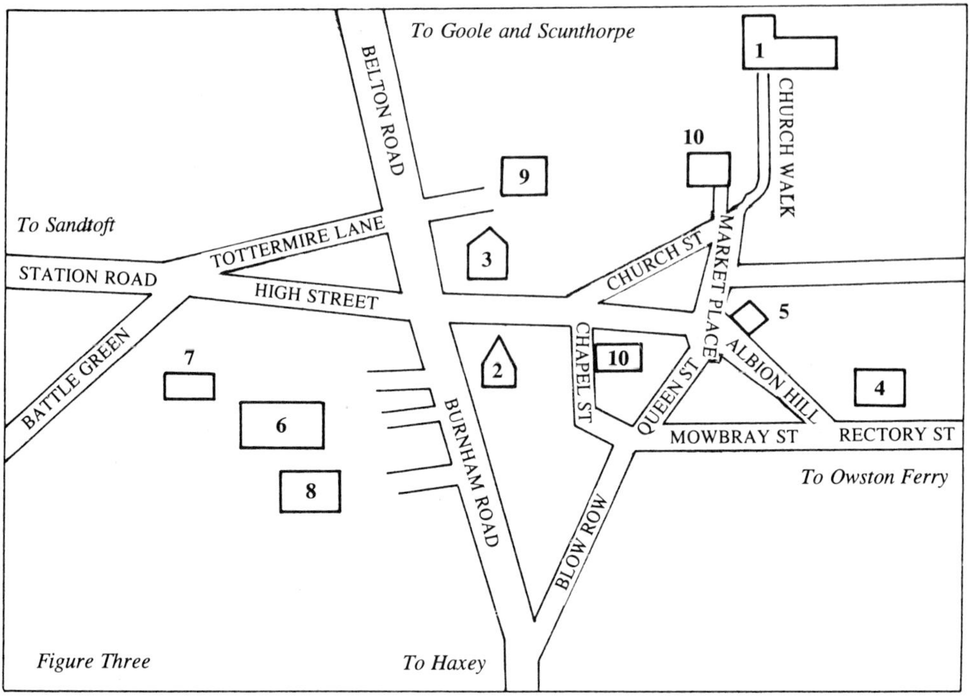

*Figure Three*

**KEY** — **SIMPLIFIED PLAN OF EPWORTH TOWN CENTRE**

1. St Andrew's Parish Church
2. Wesley Memorial Church
3. Kilham Memorial Church
4. Old Rectory, John Wesley's boyhood home.
5. The Red Lion Inn
6. Comprehensive School
7. Primary School
8. Leisure Centre
9. Garden Centre
10. Car Parks

Church Walk - the age old track to the Parish Church often used by the Wesley family. This scene was captured on film about the turn of the century.

*Courtesy Edwin Harrison.*

Wesleys. John Wesley's father lies buried here and his world famous son preached from his grave to crowds of eager listeners.(REF. 1)

The Market Place itself is still the very hub of this quaint old town; a centre that has throbbed with the hustle and bustle of trading and dealing ever since Saxon times. Looking around it now at the various period facades, the mind is easily transported to the days of mud and stud dwellings; droves of cattle and pigs; the shout of the town crier; the hoarse laughter around the stocks and pillory; the jeers and catcalls by the baited bear or bull and the tight little gathering watching the cock fighting.

Epworth's old Free School has long since disappeared, but the Church and Board Schools can still be seen as reminders of earlier educational establishments. Today's pupils are educated in a modern Primary School and a finely appointed Comprehensive School catering for children of 11 to 16 years of age from the south of the Isle of Axholme.

Industries include agriculture, agricultural engineering, manufacturing joinery and the distribution of agricultural products. Before Local Government reorganisation in 1974, Epworth was the administrative and commercial centre of the Isle of Axholme. It is still the latter, but Axholme's reign as a Rural District Council ended when it became part of Boothferry District Council based at Goole.(REF.2) In this century, residential development at Epworth has seen its population almost double as more and more people have chosen to reside in this rural area. Many people commute daily to Doncaster and Scunthorpe and other outlying destinations. To some extent this influx of newcomers has changed the nature and character of this little country town, but in the main the blend of long established residents and the newcomers is pleasantly harmonious. New houses and bungalows have filled many of the gaps featured in earlier ribbon development and reasonably attractive and tasteful residential estates have been built in areas tucked away from the town centre.

The town has police, fire and ambulance services; a library and a leisure centre and it is hoped that a swimming pool will eventually be provided. Several public houses and restaurants ensure that the visitor's appetite is well catered for and in general a visit to John Wesley's home town of Epworth can be a very enjoyable experience.

There was a time when Epworth held two annual fairs; one on the first Thursday after the 1st of May and a second on the first Thursday after the 29th of September. The town still has two great annual festive occasions being the Agricultural Show in August and the Festival of the Plough in September. The latter is a truly remarkable spectacle featuring old style ploughing methods and has achieved something of a National reputation, for it is attended by visitors countrywide.

The Draft South Axholme Development Plan in regard to Epworth has suggested that residential properties could be built on 12.3 acres south of

The Market Place looking up the road to St Andrews Church. Note London House's Victorian shop front to the right.

Epworth Old Rectory (The home of the Wesley family until 1735) and a house visited by thousands of people from all over the world.

The popular Holmes and Gardens Centre off the Belton Road. In recent years it has been enlarged and further developed and is a popular attraction for visitors from far and wide.

***Industry at Epworths old station site.*** The premises of Platts Harris in Station Road, Agricultural Machinery Dealers and Engineers and *below* the buildings of C.W. Fields and Sons who are Manufacturing Joiners.

The scene in Epworth Market Place on May 30th, 1994, for the Bienniel Wesley Day Celebrations. Children dancing around the Maypole prior to performing the Maypole dance itself.

The Rev Gordon Gatward crowns the May Queen at the 4th Bienniel Wesley day Celebrations at Epworth on Monday 30th, May 1994

Part of the delightful woodland walk around Epworth's Turbary; a Site of Special Scientific Interest. *Permission is required to enter this Nature Reserve.*

# THE FACE OF EPWORTH TODAY

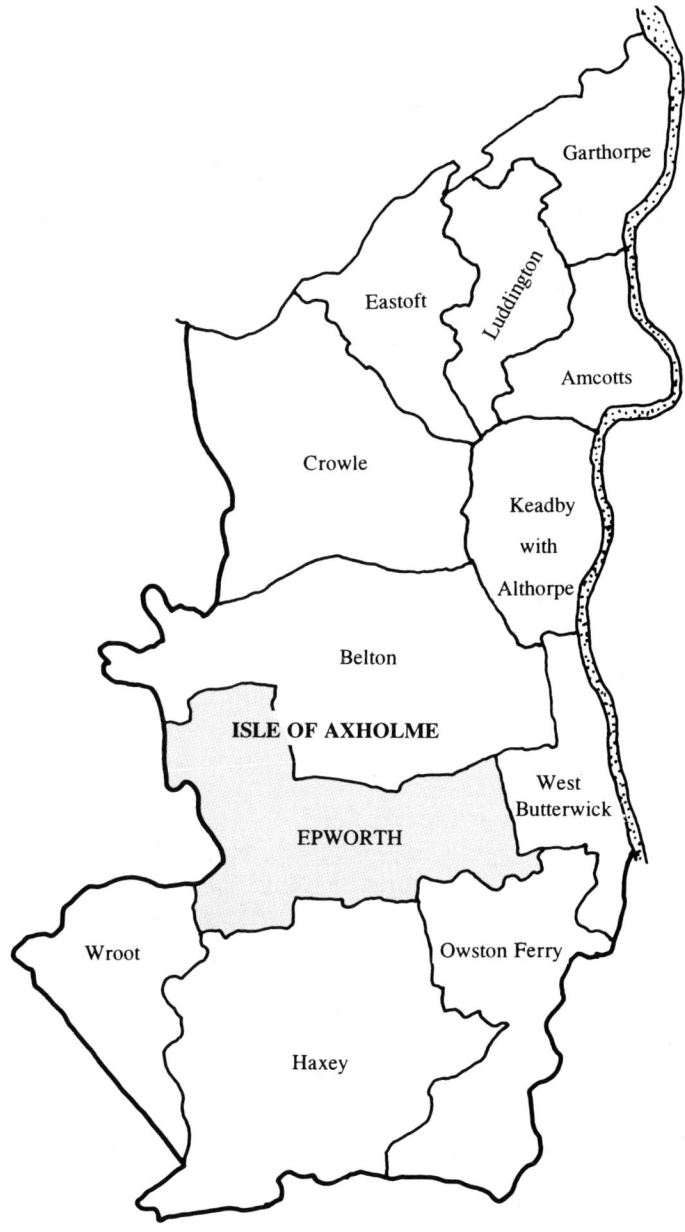

*Figure Four*

**PRESENT DAY PARISHES OF THE ISLE AXHOLME**

Mowbray Street and Rectory Street; 12.7 acres south of Battle Green and 2.5 acres off Albion Hill. This to most would seem reasonably acceptable and amenable in regard to the town's appearance.(REF.3)

A most interesting feature of the town is Mr John Harris's Haywain Farm Museum along Station Road. He has assembled a wonderful collection of wagons beautifully illustrating the art of the wainwright, and also many other items of farming memorabilia. On the occasional open days all the glory of the farming days of old are brought to life when threshing demonstrations take place and once again the blacksmith's forge roars, the sparks fly and the newly made horse shoes rattle on to the floor. In the homely setting of Fieldhouse Farm, this grand reminder of our agricultural heritage seems perfectly at home.

A later section in this book will take a further look at Epworth's streets and buildings where the ancient jostles with the present and where there is the ever pervasive sense of the past, but before we leave the modern scene, mention must be made of the town's Turbary which lies about one and half miles west of the town centre, out along the road to Wroot. It is associated with the days when villagers were allowed to dig for peat for a variety of uses, but these days it serves as one of several nature reserves in the Isle of Axholme, handled by the Lincolnshire County Trust. The 34 hectare site has been accorded the status of a Site of Special Scientific Interest (SSSI) by the Nature Conservancy Council. It has its own Warden and volunteer workers have created footpaths, rides, glades and hides, turning the area into a haven for birds, insects and small mammals. The progressive development continues at the present, but already this delightful spot reflects great credit on those who work hard to create its beauty.

The pathway at the Turbary extends around the site for some 1.3 miles and initially follows Skyers Drain along the southern edge for some 700 metres. Here a varied assortment of insects can often be seen and the trees flanking the path include alder, rowan, oak, elder, sallow, aspen, birch and hawthorn. The north bound trail is a place to look out for willow tits, long tailed tits, reed buntings and willow warblers. East bound the track crosses a ride near the power lines, a place where it is worth looking out for the green or greater spotted woodpecker. Birch is particularly prevalent in this part of the walk with clearings here and there. The final stretch of this most enjoyable stroll turns south as it skirts the woodland and in an open area may be seen wood pigeons, stockdoves, jays, magpies, yellow hammers, linnets, redpolls and green woodpeckers.(REF.4 and 5)

REFERENCES
1. *Know Your Parish.* Axholme Family History Information Sheet.
2. *Epworth Town Trail.* The Epworth Society, 1988.
3. *Boothferry Borough Local Plan.* Boothferry Borough Council, 1993.
4. *Nature Reserves Handbook.* Lincolnshire and South Humberside Trust for Nature Conservation. Second Edition, 1981.
5. Mr Geoff Trinder. Warden of Turbary Nature Reserve.

# CHAPTER TWO

## The Farm on the Hill

We turn our attention from modern Epworth to look back in an attempt to unravel some of the history of this age old capital of Axholme. The place names of the area are much the same as they were prior to the Norman conquest and Epworth is no exception. It is of interest that Eminson's *'The Place Names and River Names of West Lindsey'* lists no less than twelve different spellings for Epworth during its history. J.K.Johnstone suggests that 'Ep', the Anglo Saxon for the aspen tree and 'worth' meaning a farm, estate or manor, give the derivation of Epworth.(REF.1) The more commonly accepted meaning is that found in W.B.Stonehouse's *'History of Axholme'*. He states that the Saxon 'Heape' means a small hill and that 'urde' means a farm, and joined together they form Heapeurde, giving the rather charming designation of the'Farm on the Hill'.(REF.2)

Such a name seems entirely in keeping with the Epworth of centuries ago (before the Conquest) and it is not difficult to imagine the little group of wooden dwellings, a granary, workshops, a Headman's home and perhaps even a wooden church, all of which may have stood in Saxon Epworth. It is also highly likely that the village was positioned somewhere in the area of the present parish church or market place and that today's town has grown out from this settlement.

Although we can talk of a Saxon settlement with some certainty this is not to suggest that Axholme did not have its inhabitants thousands of years earlier. The old World War II observer post to the north east of the church is said to be on the site of an Iron Age settlement.( REF.3) This is where the archaeologist comes to our aid and several years ago a team from the Humberside County Council Archaeology Unit carried out a number of field walking exercises in the Isle of Axholme to look for evidence of early settlements. This kind of examination of arable fields can prove informative, for pottery sherds, worked flints and small metal finds can reveal a great deal about the peoples of the past.

A survey team walked over thirty fields in the Isle of Axholme and in addition to finds in other areas, coins of the Roman and Tudor periods; flints, sherds and axe heads were discovered within the Epworth Parish. The flint blades, cores, flakes, scrapers and arrow heads dated from 4000 to 2000BC as well as from the later Bronze Age and the sherds were examples of Romano-British greyware pottery.(REF.4)

Substantial quantities of Roman pottery had been revealed earlier on low lying land near Crowle and proved to be the shiny, red Samian ware imported from Gaul between the first and second centuries AD. There may have been a greater degree of settlement in Celtic and Roman times in the Isle of Axholme than has usually been believed. Excavations at nearby Sandtoft in 1975 revealed a Romano-British settlement on the former course of the River Idle. The dig

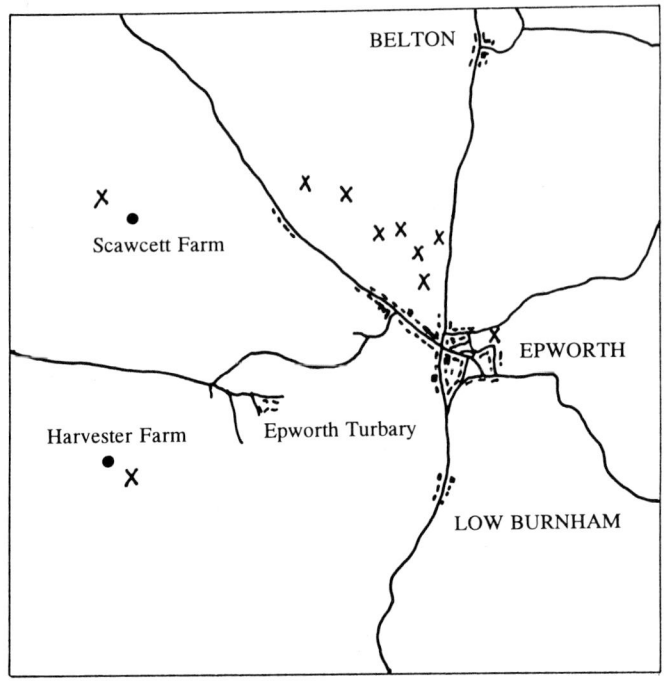

*Figure Five*     **FLINT DISCOVERIES IN THE EPWORTH PARISH**

The crosses indicate approximations to areas in which flint discoveries were made by the Humberside Archaeology Unit's Isle of Axholme Survey Team in Fieldwalking exercises in the late 1980's. Flint flakes, implements, blades, cores and scrapers were unearthed dating from the neolithic period of around 4000 to 2000 BC.

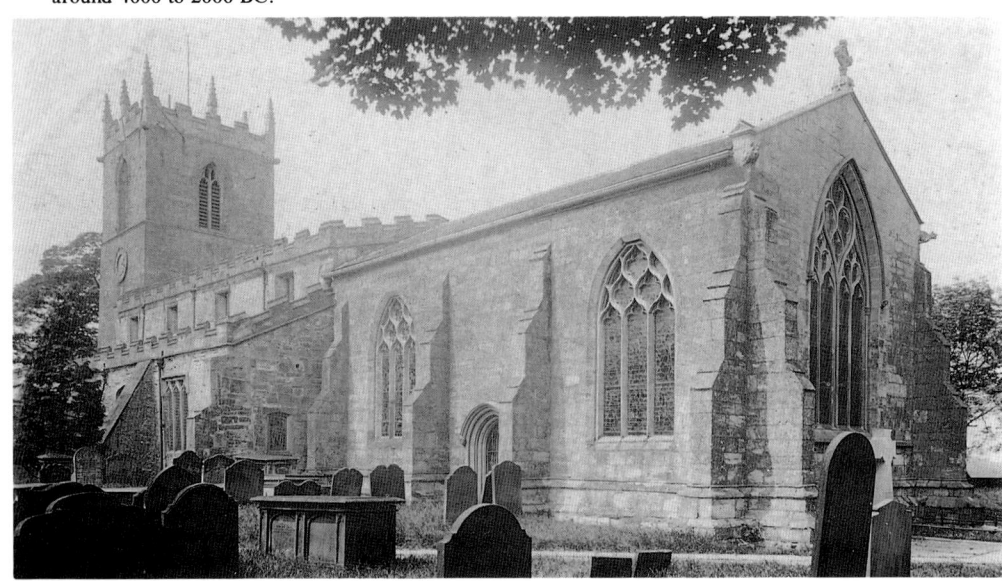

A commercial postcard view of St Andrews Church, Epworth showing clearly the different periods of construction that the church has gone through.

*Rural Publications*

discovered that two roundhouses had probably stood on the river bank and that grain was being stored nearby.

The minor road network built by the Romans perhaps deserves greater attention and if they did provide any west to east route between Doncaster and Ermine Street it is possible that the Epworth area may have been a settlement along it. In regard to even earlier settlement nearby Belton might indicate that Druidism existed there in Celtic times. The many 'Bel' prefixes (the God of the Sun, fertility and fire ) seen in Beltoft, Belshaw, Temple Belwood and the Belgraves, would suggest the practice of this ancient religion.

However, the first sure reference to Epworth is recorded in the Doomsday record where we see that, 'In Epeurde Ledwin had eight carucates of land rateable to gelt; the land is twelve carucates. Geoffrey de Wirce has there two carucates (in demesne), and eight sokemen with two carucates and five bovates of this land and thirteen villeins and nine bordars with six carucates, and eleven fisheries worth 5s. yearly, and sixteen acres of meadow. There is a wood containing pasturage a mile long and a mile broad. The annual value in King Edward's time was 8L; it is now 5L. It is tallaged at 20s.(REF.5)

Readers may find some explanation of some of the Doomsday terms helpful and in regard to the carucate; in Lincolnshire, it is usually regarded as around 120 acres. Gelt means tax; a bovate was an eighth of a carucate; a Sokeman was a free peasant liable to attend the Court of his Soke and to serve his Lord; the villein was the highest ranking dependent peasant owing his Lord duties and services in return for his land; bordars (from the Saxon 'bord', a cottage); cottagers - small plot owners and finally tallage was the tax levied by a Lord from his tenants.

With the carucate representing 120 acres this would have given Epworth, at that time, an arable land acreage of 1440 acres, plus woodland of 640 acres and also what seems rather small in proportion, sixteen acres of meadow. We can also roughly calculate the population at this time as the survey mentions 32 people, and if we estimate that families may have consisted of five people each, then Epworth could have had a population of around 160. A similar calculation for Haxey gives 130; for Upperthorpe 170; Crowle 175 and Owston 80. It gives 225 for Belton, but this is explained by the fact that Belton is the only place in Axholme reported as possessing two manors. Given that the population of Lincolnshire was estimated in the 11th century at 126,525, then the Isle of Axholme figure of roughly 1415 would seem to be in proportion.

This then is what the Norman assessors found at the 'farm on the hill' and even then it seems to have been one of the richest parts of Axholme. The Conqueror's survey gives the impression that Saxon Axholme had developed into a reasonably profitable arable, pasture, fishing and fowling area. The Normans would have found a village administered under the usual Anglo Saxon system of government. Any village containing at least ten families had a Headborough and ten such

*Figure Six*

**ARCHAEOLOGICAL FINDS IN AXHOLME**

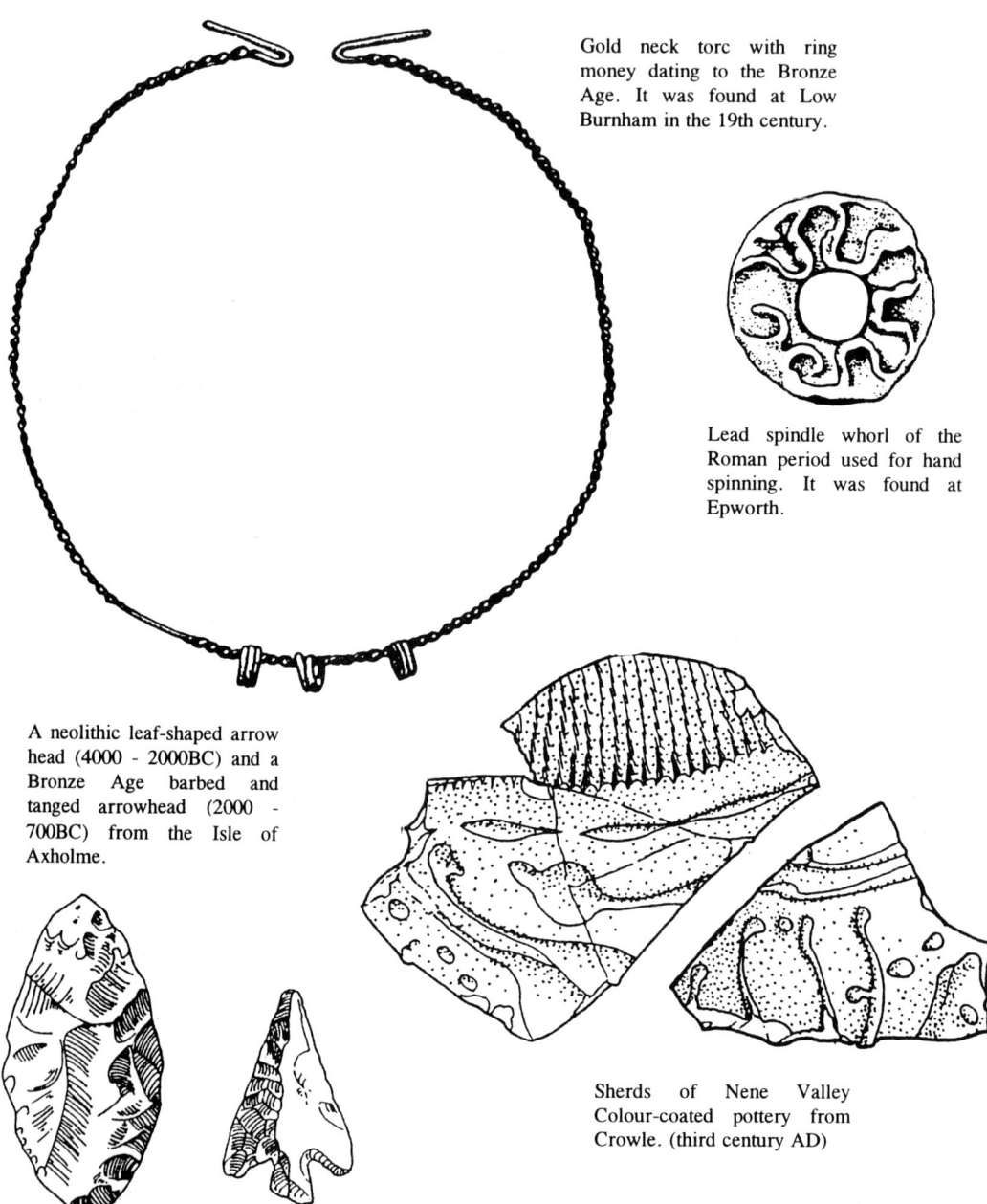

Gold neck torc with ring money dating to the Bronze Age. It was found at Low Burnham in the 19th century.

Lead spindle whorl of the Roman period used for hand spinning. It was found at Epworth.

A neolithic leaf-shaped arrow head (4000 - 2000BC) and a Bronze Age barbed and tanged arrowhead (2000 - 700BC) from the Isle of Axholme.

Sherds of Nene Valley Colour-coated pottery from Crowle. (third century AD)

*Illustrations by permission of the Humberside Archaeology Unit.*

villages formed a Hundred (usually termed a Wapentake) with a presiding officer known as a hundreder. Axholme, along with some villages east of the River Trent formed the Manley Hundred.

The Doomsday account mentions only Crowle and Haxey as possessing churches, but this in itself would seem to indicate that the influence of the Christian missionaries in the north of England had penetrated Axholme. It is significant that the churches of Crowle, Luddington and Althorpe are all named after the saintly Christian King Oswald and it seems highly likely that wooden churches would have existed in several areas of Axholme well before the Conquest - including Epworth.

Everywhere the growth of the Anglo Saxon villages was accompanied by the development of the open-field system - at its earliest, mostly consisting of one large field. Through the twenty generations of Anglo-Saxon settlement the acreage of the utilised land grew larger and larger as wild land and woodland was cleared for cultivation. For centuries the unit of cultivation was to become the strip or selion, and a parcel of such, all running in the same direction made up what was known as a furlong. As Axholme still retains one of the finest examples of the open-field system in England, we shall examine it further in a later chapter.

Finally Axholme's strategic defence position may also have contributed to a concentration of settlers in the Epworth area. The district had a unique defensive setting for it formed, at various times a gateway, a frontier or fortress. In Romano-British times it was the northern extremity of the Coritani territory, the ancient inhabitants of Lincolnshire. Later still it was the stormy frontier of Northern Mercia (an area of constant friction) and adjacent to Northumbria. Central in this strategic buffer zone was the Epworth settlement and it was here that William the Conqueror established his henchmen to rule Axholme.

REFERENCES
1. Johnstone, J.K. *The Isle of Axholme. Its Place Names and River Names.* Foster Barnes. Epworth 1886.
2. Stonehouse, W.B. *The History and Topography of the Isle of Axholme.* Longman, Rees, Orme and Company, 1839.
3. *Epworth Town Trail.* 1988.
4. *Isle of Axholme Survey.* Bulletin Number 3, 1988. Humberside Archaeology Unit.
5. Smith, C.G. *Doomsday Book which relates to Lincolnshire and Rutlandshire.* J.Williamson and George Gale, 1870.

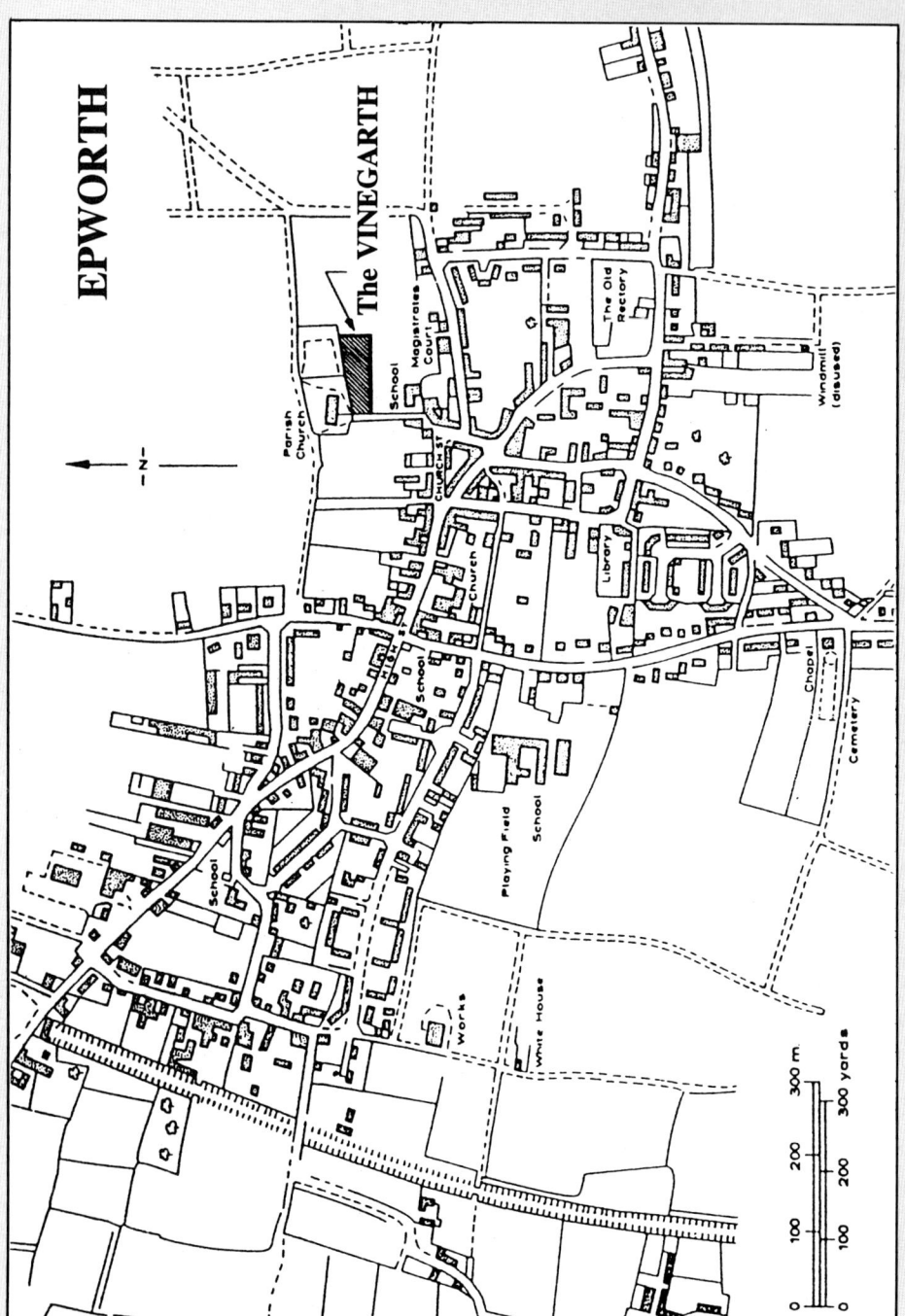

*Figure Seven*
**THE POSITION OF THE VINEGARTH IN RELATION TO EPWORTH TOWN**
*Source : Lincolnshire History and Archaeology. Vol 19, 1984 - used with permission.*

# CHAPTER THREE

## The Mowbray Period

William the Conqueror gave the whole of Axholme, as well as many other possessions to Geoffrey de Wirce. This powerful Baron had numerous lands in Warwickshire and Leicestershire, and Epworth was but one of his twenty-four Lordships in Lincolnshire. It included the Manors of Epworth, Belton, Haxey, Owston, Crowle, Luddington, Burnham, Lound and Wroot. When de Wirce died leaving no issue, his possessions reverted to the Crown, but were later bestowed on Nigel d'Albini, a former bow-bearer to William Rufus, but in this second grant, the Manor of Crowle and virtually northern Axholme was given to the Abbot of Selby.

There were two sons from d'Albini's second marriage, Roger and Henry. The former assumed by Royal Mandate, the name of Mowbray and this is where the associations of that famous name began in Axholme. Roger de Mowbray led a rebellion against Henry II but Geoffrey, the King's eldest son brought his father's forces into Axholme and forced the Mowbray Castle at Owston Ferry to surrender through lack of water and this fortress was then demolished. Roger repented of his action and was afterwards firm in his allegiance to Henry II.

The charities of this Norman overlord were numerous and locally they included the appropriation of the churches of Haxey, Owston, Epworth and Belton to the Abbey of Newburgh, itself founded by Roger de Mowbray. He also established Byland Abbey and a Preceptory in Warwickshire was endowed with certain lands in the Isle, whilst Sandtoft was given to the Abbey of St Mary at York.

The Mowbray house at Epworth was probably built as early as the 12th century and was situated in the Vine Garth near the church - the land nearby being ideally suited to grape growing, and vineyards were a popular innovation of the time. To the south of their Epworth home the Mowbrays also took for their own use and pleasure the fields and woods that were later to become the vast and beautiful Belgrave Park.

Roger de Mowbray, whilst on the Crusades, was imprisoned by Saladin, ransomed by the Templars, but died abroad. His son, Nigel, also set out for battle in the Holy Land, but died in 1191 before arriving there. He left four sons; William, Robert, Philip and Roger. The eldest, William, played a prominent part in compelling King John to sign the Magna Carta; then plotted with Louis of France against Henry III and was imprisoned. The King accepted his submission and William retired to Axholme where he died in 1222 at his Vine Garth home, but he was buried at Newburgh.(REF.1)

William's two sons played little part in the affairs of State, Nigel dying in Brittany in 1228, and his brother Roger breathed his last at the Mowbray Manor in Epworth, but not before he had fathered six sons and three daughters. His

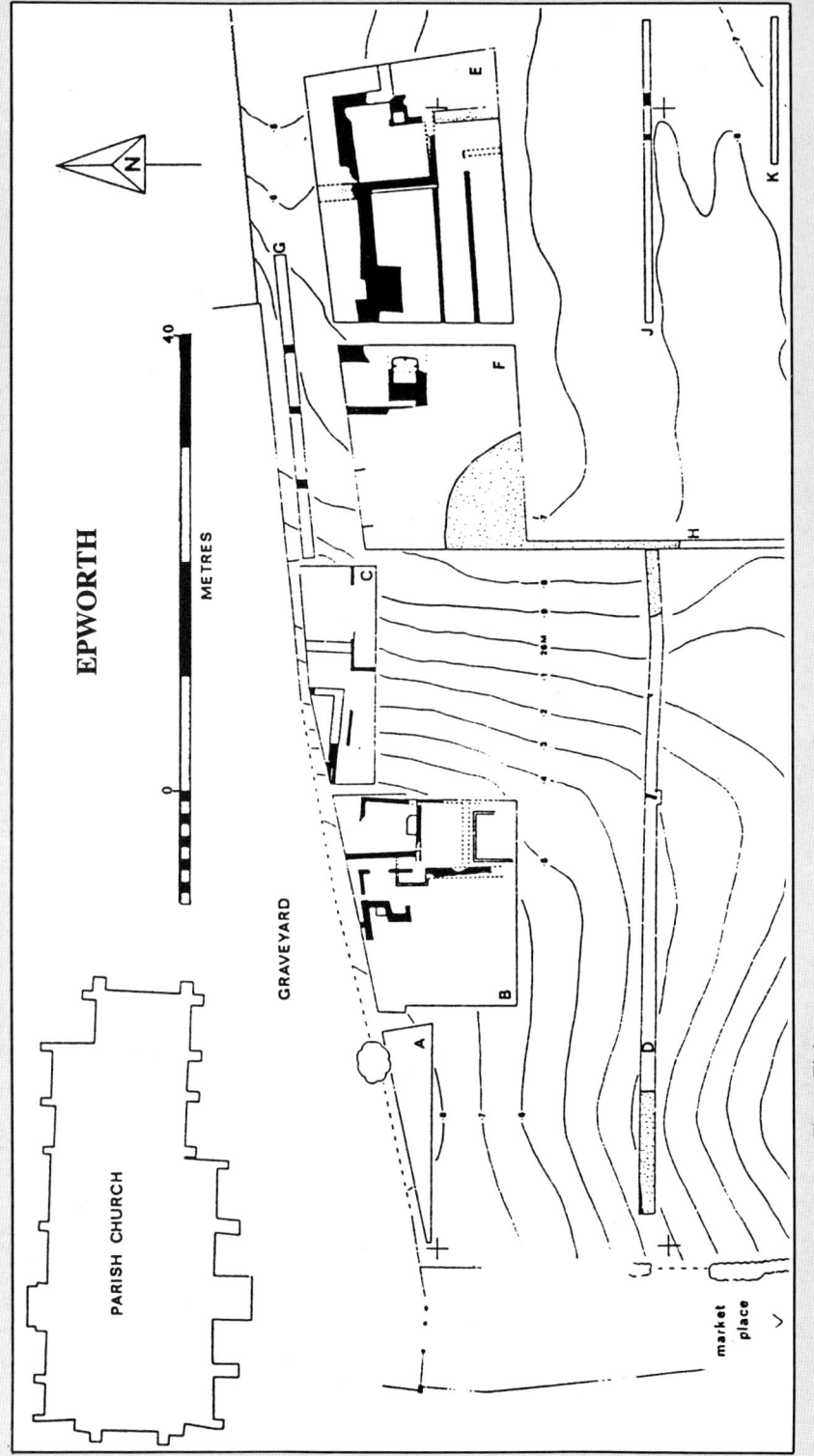

*Figure Eight*
**LOCATION DIAGRAM OF THE EXCAVATED TRENCHES WITHIN THE VINEGARTH**
*See Table One for explanations of findings*

*Source - Lincolnshire History and Archaeology Vol 19 184 - used with permission*

# THE MOWBRAY PERIOD

**TABLE ONE**
Detail of Trench Excavation at the Vinegarth at Epworth in relation to *Figure 8*

| Trench letter | Principal features of discovery |
|---|---|
| A | Possible ancillary building |
| B | 1. Quarry dug to 1.40m.<br>2. Cesspit and two other pits<br>3. Two rooms with passage - possibly two further rooms. Early walls of red and green marlstone bonded with brown marl clay. Later walls of the same material, but mixed with bricks and sandstone and bonded with red and green marl clay and brown, chalk flecked clay.<br>4. Lean-to with water cistern 0.80m in diameter.<br>5. Northern wall of a timber-framed construction. |
| C | 1. Possible early graveyard wall to north west - 0.30m in height.<br>2. Flat marlstone floor in angle of two walls.<br>3. Wide wall to the north with a water cistern with conduit on each side. |
| D | Massive amount of demolition material at two metres. Possible range of buildings fronting either side of the track to the church. |
| E | 1. Main Manorial Hall of 16 metres in length. Possible foundations of external staircase to upper chamber.<br>2. Two phase kitchen - later one with two hearths. Floor of bricks and tiles - many of the latter showing the Mowbray Arms. |
| F | 1. West wall of Hall<br>2. Probable base of garderobe tower servicing the hall at first floor level. |
| G | Exploratory |
| H | Demolition Material |
| J and K | Traces of parallel walls - possible covered walkway. |

A further view of St Andrews Church, Epworth taken at the turn of the Century and reproduced from a booklet issued in 1905 by the Lancashire & Yorkshire Railway, entitled :- *Epworth - What to see and How to Get There.*   *Courtesy of Miss Marjorie Trimingham*

eldest son, Roger died at Ghent, but was buried at Fountains Abbey. Roger's eldest son, John, carried on the Mowbray line in the Isle of Axholme, but was hanged in 1321 for his part in a rebellion against Edward II's High Chamberlain. His wife and son were imprisoned in the Tower of London and once again the Manors of the Mowbrays in Axholme were confiscated by the Crown.

When Edward III came to the throne, he released Roger's wife and son John and restored to the latter, the lands forfeited by his father's rebellion. John was made Governor of Berwick-on-Tweed and distinguished himself in the King's service in battles at home and abroad. He died of the plague in 1361 and was succeeded by his son, also named John, who was to become by far the best known Overlord in Axholme for it was he who issued the renowned Mowbray Deed which gave his subjects in the Isle of Axholme free use of the common land in the various manors. This Baron had himself incurred the grievances of his tenants by his own use of common land and made redress by establishing this legal charter, mainly for the benefit of the occupiers of common land. (REF.2)

It is of interest to set out some of the provisions of this celebrated document written originally in French and signed on 1st May, 1360. It bound all future Lords of the Epworth Manor to permit certain benefits in perpetuity. Bearing this in mind, no wonder there was great unrest and ensuing violence following Vermuyden's rough shod disregard of these provisions, when he undertook his drainage scheme.

Amongst the Rights granted to the freeholders was the privilege to dig on the moors and marshes, turf, trees and roots; to dig turf for the walls of their houses and yards and to make tiles for roof covering. They were allowed to fell trees for the banking of the River Trent and also allowed various waters for the retting of hemp. There were other privileges, but the main import of this document was the granting of the use of the commons to Axholme's tenant farmers. John de Mowbray did apportion part of the common land for himself, but all future Lords were debarred from taking any further parts - a principal that was the basis of the Commoner's case against Vermuyden's claim on their commons at the time of the drainage and later. (REF.3)

The son of the Mowbray Deed's author, John, was born at Epworth in 1365 and later succeeded his father. At the Coronation of Richard II in 1377 he was created Earl of Nottingham. He died in 1382 in London and his brother Thomas inherited his title and lands, and three years later became the Earl Marshall of England for life.

Thomas de Mowbray is remembered for his founding of the Carthusian Monastery at Low Melwood, one of only nine of this order in the country. In 1397 he became the Duke of Norfolk, but shortly afterwards he was accused of plotting against Richard II and was banished, dying in Venice in 1399. A few years later Henry IV gave permission for his body to be brought back to England and Thomas was laid to rest at Low Melwood in the Monastery he had founded.

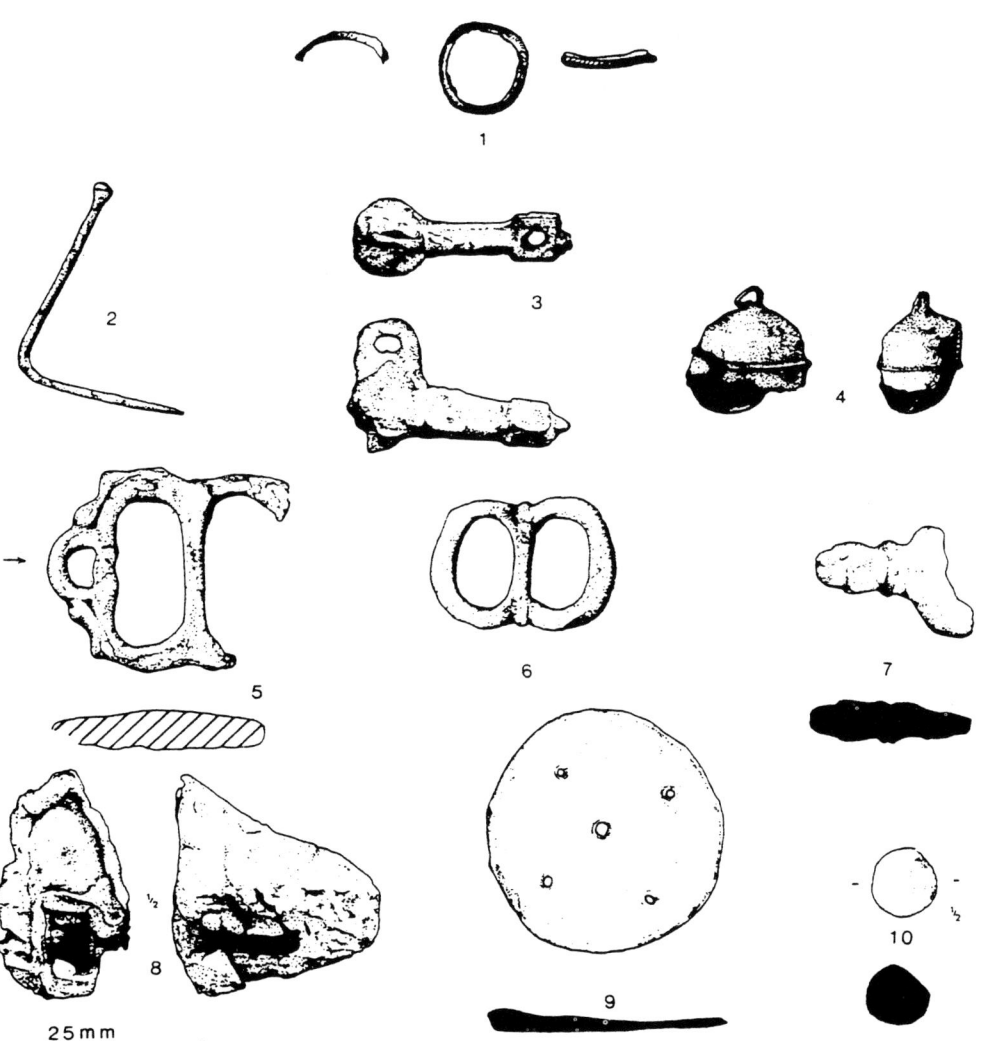

*Figure Nine*
Small finds at the Vinegarth Excavations, Epworth 1975/76. Small objects discovered were coins, a bronze candlestick and many other objects of copper-alloy, silver, lead or iron. Some are pictured above and their explanations are given below.

1. Silver wire ring. Trench E
2. Copper-alloy pin. Trench C
3. Possible parts of set of scales. Trench C
4. Small beaten bell. Trench A
5. Decorative Cast belt buckle. Trench B
6. Small Plain buckle. Trench C
7. Fragment from a key. Trench D
8. Plugs of lead. Trench C
9. Small Strainer. Trench C
10. Lead Musket Balls. Trench C

*Source :* Lincolnshire History and Archaeology. Vol 19, 1984.     *Reproduced with permission.*

Thomas de Mowbray's son of the same name followed his father's plotting and with several others tried to dethrone Henry IV. He was taken prisoner by the Earl of Westmorland and beheaded in 1405. He was succeeded by his brother, John, who fought with Henry V at Harfleur, but returned to England because of illness before the famous battle at Agincourt. In 1425 Henry VI restored him to the title of Duke of Norfolk. He died in 1433 and was buried with his family in the Chapter House of Melwood Monastery. (REF.4)

The next Mowbray Baron, another John, filled numerous high diplomatic positions under Henry VI and was ultimately given that of Justice Itinerant of all the Forests south of the Trent. As he died in 1461, the year of his appointment, it is unlikely that he ever carried out this task! His son and heir (yet another John) brought the Mowbray influence in Axholme to an end and the honours and inheritance of this noble family passed into the hands of the families of Howard and Berkeley. William, Marquis of Berkeley having no successor, settled much of his property on Henry VII and this monarch gave him leave to dispose of twenty-five of his Lordships as he pleased. The outcome of this was that he sold his Axholme possessions in Epworth, Belton, Haxey, Owston and Wroot to Thomas Standing, the Earl of Derby. (REF.5)

One has to marvel at the amount of work achieved in England by the Normans. Apart from the construction of numerous strongholds, they established churches built of stone in every county - not just here and there, but literally everywhere. Here in Axholme churches were well established at Haxey, Owston, Belton, Wroot, Crowle and Luddington. The community of Epworth, like others in Axholme, would be taking shape and the rough tracks around St Andrew's Church, the Vine Garth and the Market Place, may well have approximated to the present road layout.

The Mowbrays kept law and order through the Court Baron and Court Leet and the conjunction of these courts gave the Lord supreme power, allowing him to impose even the death penalty for what we today would regard as petty crime. The Court Leet at Epworth still functioned in the second half of the last century as a unit of local government, regulating the drainage of a considerable area of Axholme and preserving the boundaries of the open-field system. It was the Manorial Court which gave the Commoners the right of pasturage in all the commons, for all sorts of cattle, at all times of the year and common turbary to dig wood, sand, sods and clay for any purpose.

As the historian Read logically comments, "One would think that the Isle Commoners had overlooked the rights conferred by the Court, or they would have had some better ground to depend on, if such could be, than the Mowbray Deed, in their disputes with Vermuyden and his participants". (REF.6)

The Mowbrays served Axholme well and their organisation established a firm foundation for later social, agricultural and commercial development. Many of them were held in high esteem by England's monarchs whilst others were notable for trying to oust them. Their Coat of Arms with the lion rampant well reflects the many strong qualities of this historic family.

Before we leave the Mowbrays it seems appropriate to consider the excavations which were carried out at Epworth in 1975 and 1976 on the Vine Garth site. When Boothferry District Council declared their intention to build a residential estate in the arable field, known as the Vine Garth, the Ancient Monuments Inspectorate of the Department of the Environment financed two seasons of excavations on the site under the direction of Mr R.A.H.Williams.

The archaeological dig quickly proved that the Vine Garth was the site of an extensive range of buildings dating from the 14th to 16th centuries. The discovery of a tile floor in situ bearing the Arms of the Mowbrays, gave little doubt that the buildings did comprise the ancient Manor House of that family. *Figure 7* shows the position of the Vine Garth in relation to Epworth town and *Figure 8* indicates the positions of the various exploratory trenches used in examining the area. It is not my intention here to give detailed accounts of the findings, but *Table 1* will give the reader a useful guide to the scope of the project. It has to be said that *Figure 8* may by no means reveal anything like the full extent of the Mowbray house which could well have been much larger and grander, and very much in keeping with the status of such a distinguished family.

As would be expected in an exploration of this nature many examples of medieval and post-medieval pottery were found which had originated from kilns at Doncaster, Beverley, West Cowick and Conisborough. There were also numerous small sherds from kilns at Scarborough, Hedon, Lincoln and Nottingham, as well as examples of German stoneware and pottery of French and Dutch origin.(REF.7)

REFERENCES
1. Stonehouse, W.B.  (1839) op.cit.
2. Ibid.
3. Read , W.    *History of the Isle of Axholme, its Manors and Parishes.*
      Fletcher,T.C. (ed) Epworth, 1858.
4. Stonehouse, W.B.  (1839) op.cit.
5. Ibid.
6. Read. W.  (1858) op.cit.
7. Hayfield, Colin.   *Excavations on the site of the Mowbray Manor House at Vinegarth, Epworth. Lincolnshire, 1975 and 1976.*
      Lincolnshire History and Archaeology. Vol.19,1984.

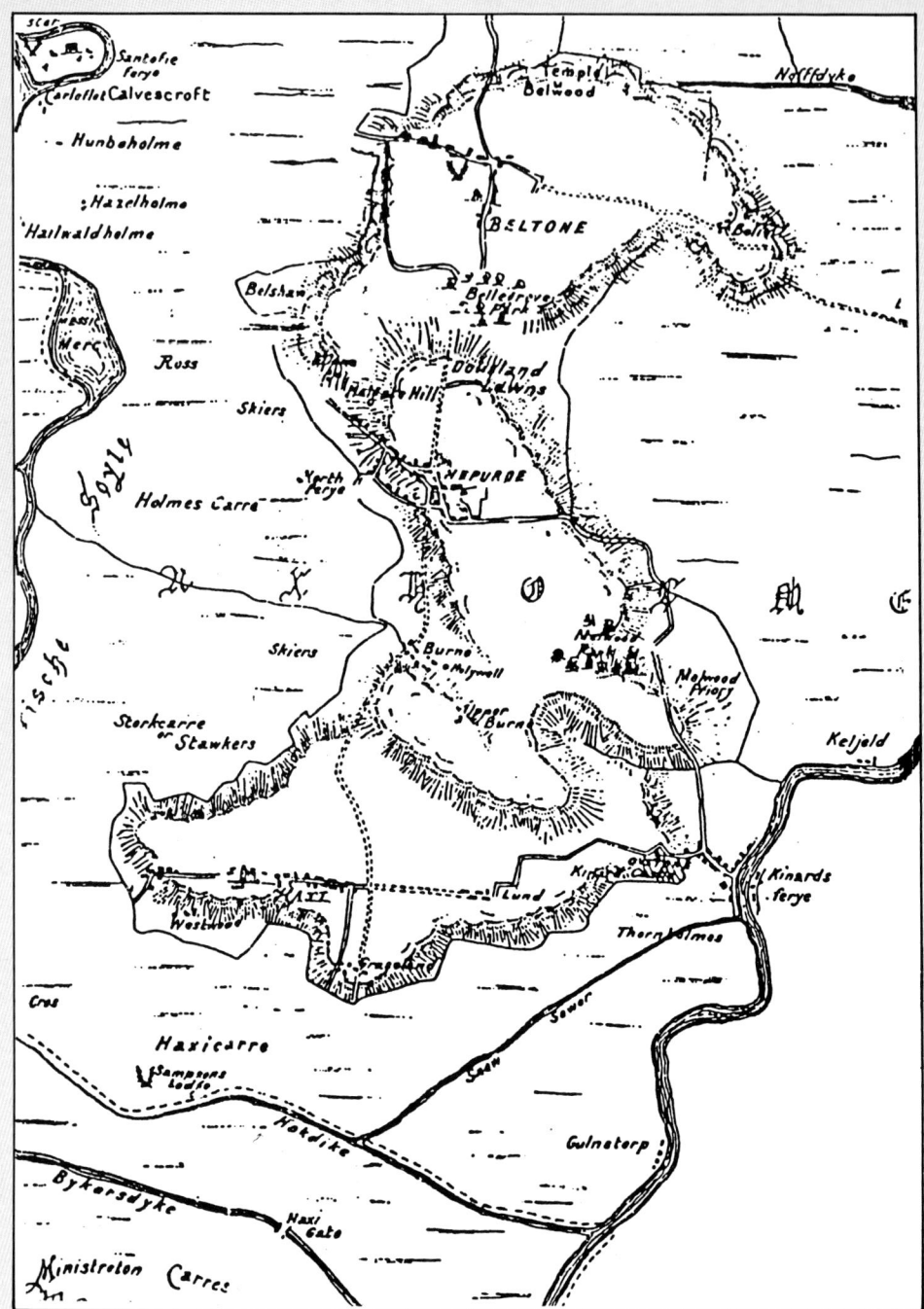

*Figure Ten.* **THE ISLE OF AXHOLME IN THE EARLY 16th CENTURY**

A section from a map dated 1526 found in Tomlinson's History of Hatfield Chace and which shows Epworth (here spelt HEPURDE) and its surrounds before the drainage of a century later. Here one can immediately see why Axholme is termed an Isle.

# CHAPTER FOUR

## Town Development and Drainage Squabbles

Part of a 1526 map of Hatfield Chace is shown in *figure 10* and is useful for the purpose of looking at Epworth around that period of time. The town is then referred to as Hepurde and even then we can see roadway development in line with that of today. There is roadway connection with 'Kinard's Ferye' to the south east, but southwards to Haxey there would have appeared to have been only rough track links and the same applies northwards to Belton. It can clearly be seen that the area is indeed an isle surrounded by fenland; Haxey Carr to the south, Holmes Carr to the west with the marshlands to the north and low lying swamp land to the east

The ribbon development of that time is consequently on the east to west road (a logical layout for it) as it is likely that Epworth's trading connections would have been with Thorne and Doncaster westwards and Owston Ferry to the east, this latter to make use of transport on the Trent. We can only guess at the probable quality of these rough and narrow routes. The Church preached that repairing roads was a pious work and they urged the faithful to leave legacies for mending the roads. The inhabitants of monasteries also repaired roads and Melwood Priory may have played some part in maintaining the road between Owston and Epworth, if only to look after the interest of its own visitors. Many early roads in towns and villages were provided by private benefactors. The General Highways Act of 1555 required that the inhabitants of every parish should work for 4 days of each year on road repairs under the supervision of their own appointed surveyors, a business which was later transferred to the Justices. This scheme was not very popular and many people refused to do this work, but nevertheless it survived for three centuries before its abolition in 1823.

A closer look at the Hatfield Chace map shows housing development around the market place and such village growth can also be seen around the centres of Owston, Haxey, and Belton. The estate of the Lord of the Manor would have been enclosed in what is called Dousland Lawns and Bellegreve Park. The place marked North Ferye west of Epworth suggests that people needed to travel by boat at times in order to reach Wroot, Sandtoft and Thorne.

Although bricks would certainly have been coming into use, most properties would still have been of the wooden frame variety with the pans infilled with split laths or wattle and covered with a mixture of straw, mud or dung. This was sometimes covered with whitewash or colourwash to make the exterior more attractive. Box-frame constructions made possible upper rooms and in Tudor times these would have appeared in Epworth. Thatch roofs were in wide use until the end of the 16th century and Stonehouse comments that Beltoft contained only a few large thatched houses in 1839, seeming to indicate that all that Hamlet's

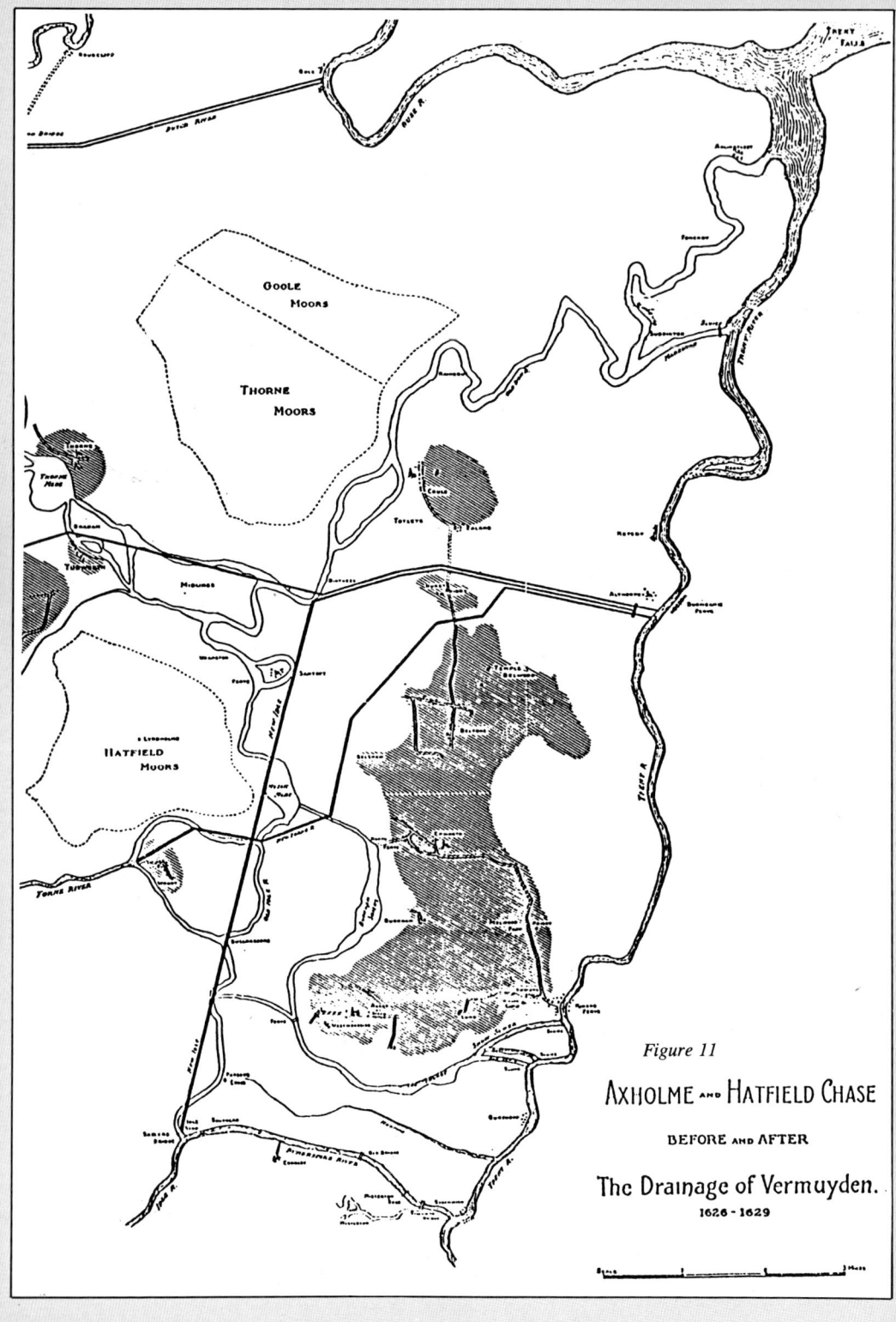

Figure 11

AXHOLME AND HATFIELD CHASE

BEFORE AND AFTER

The Drainage of Vermuyden.

1626 - 1629

roofs were then thatched. Epworth had thatch roof properties in Victorian times and one or two even into the present century. Roof material varied consisting of straw, reeds, heather, turf, moss or even flax. A rye strawthatch could last for thirty years, but reed roofs could remain good for a hundred years.

Some houses in Epworth would undoubtedly have been stone or brick-built by the 16th century, as brick manufacturing was then becoming a rapidly growing industry. Bricks had been made in Axholme and the surrounding district from the middle ages and 14th century Hull was the first town to be built of brick. More and more constructions were erected, but bricks were still expensive for the ordinary house.

It is unlikely that glass windows were much seen in Epworth at this early period, perhaps existing in the church, manor house, and some of the homes of the gentry. Many window holes would perhaps have been covered with oiled fabric, parchment, thin horn and in some cases even animal placentas, all of which let in a little light. Some homes would have had enclosed fireplaces, and chimney stacks built of brick, began to be added at the gable end of timber-framed houses and also up through the centre to emerge in what were termed axial chimneys. Houses were also beginning to feature cooking bars, pots, spits and bread ovens.

In regard to agriculture the Normans had improved and enlarged the groundwork of the Saxons and the Isle had been developed into a well cultivated district. The reasonably balanced economy continued into the 16th century with pasture producing meat and dairy produce and arable land giving a good yield of barley and wheat, with an ever increasing acreage put aside for hemp and flax.

The central ridge of fertile land running the length of Axholme from north to south then occupied about a quarter of its total area and in 1603 the main settlements of Crowle, Belton, Haxey and Epworth each contained over 150 families, again giving some very rough guide to population. It was a largely peasant community, but they were coping well and working to achieve a reasonable standard of life from the tilled land, pasture, marshes and fens around them.

This quiet rural scene knew nothing of Charles I's desire to reclaim arable land by the draining of the fenland. Royalty had been eyeing the possibility of agricultural development in Hatfield Chace and Axholme for many years and when it came to the crunch, the settled and fairly contented life style in Axholme was ignored. In 1626 a contract to carry out drainage operations in Hatfield Chace and Axholme was given to the Dutch drainage engineer, Cornelius Vermuyden.

The commons of the area were under pressure long before Vermuyden started his drainage scheme and there was a large acreage of good common pasture between Hatfield Chace and the Epworth Manor. When the Dutchman started his work this common land was included in his reclamation and Epworth Manor was particularly affected, *Figure 12* illustrating the area over which there arose years and years of bitter protest. It was in Axholme's central districts of Epworth and Belton that the strongest feelings were aroused.

The common land to the west of Epworth was a valuable asset in spite of flooding problems. In the Epworth and Westwood Manor 12,000 cattle were kept during the winter months- housed and yarded on the higher ground, but put out to graze very rich pasture on common land in the summertime. Fens and meres also provided ample fishing and fowling and local turbaries provided an abundance of peat. There was even a thriving trade in the movement of peat in the long narrow boats which took this cargo *via* the River Idle and the Don out to Turnbridge, where it was transferred to barges which carried it to the River Aire or the Ouse and on to various northern towns.(REF.1)

Under Vermuyden's Drainage scheme former common land used as pasture was offered back to Axholme farmers as arable land, but this was not an attractive proposition, especially as they were offered only a third of the acreage which they considered their rightful possession. They believed that the King had no power to dispose of their common granted by the Mowbray Deed of 1360. A great scheme like the drainage operation was certain to affect adversely some land owners, but there can be little doubt that Vermuyden pursued his task in a manner that often amounted to injustice. One writer has said that the charge that the Isleonians were stubborn and ignorant should really have been levelled at the insensitive and unjust Parliament and Crown that was utterly ignorant of the conditions around Axholme.(REF.2)

Retaliation was no surprise and the Commoners of Epworth and the surrounding areas soon registered their anger both by lawful and unlawful methods. As soon as the Dutch engineers set about their work the locals of Axholme made frequent assaults on the drainage sites, destroying banks, sluices and machinery. Some of the rioters were arrested and had to pay heavy fines.

Further unrest occurred when the Isle men claimed rights of common on 13,400 acres on Epworth South Moor and Butterwick Moor. A Commission headed by Sir John Banks met in 1636 and awarded 7,000 acres to the Commoners, and the Participants were ordered to pay £400 in compensation to enable poor folk in Epworth, Belton and Owston to buy material to make sackcloth and cordage. Not satisfied with this award, disgruntled Isleonians again attacked the foreign workers, throwing some of them into the River Torne and also destroying more banks, filling up ditches and burning tools. Four Epworth men, John Moody, Hezekiah Brown, William Torksey and Henry Scott, were arrested and were sentenced to pillory punishment and heavy fines. It appears they were bought off by the generosity of their friends and they eluded the shame of the pillory.(REF.3)

When the Civil War broke out in 1642 the Isleonians, not unnaturally, took the side of the Parliamentarians whilst the settlers supported the Royalists. John Hamilton's fictional works, *'The Manuscript in the Red Box'* and *'Captain John*

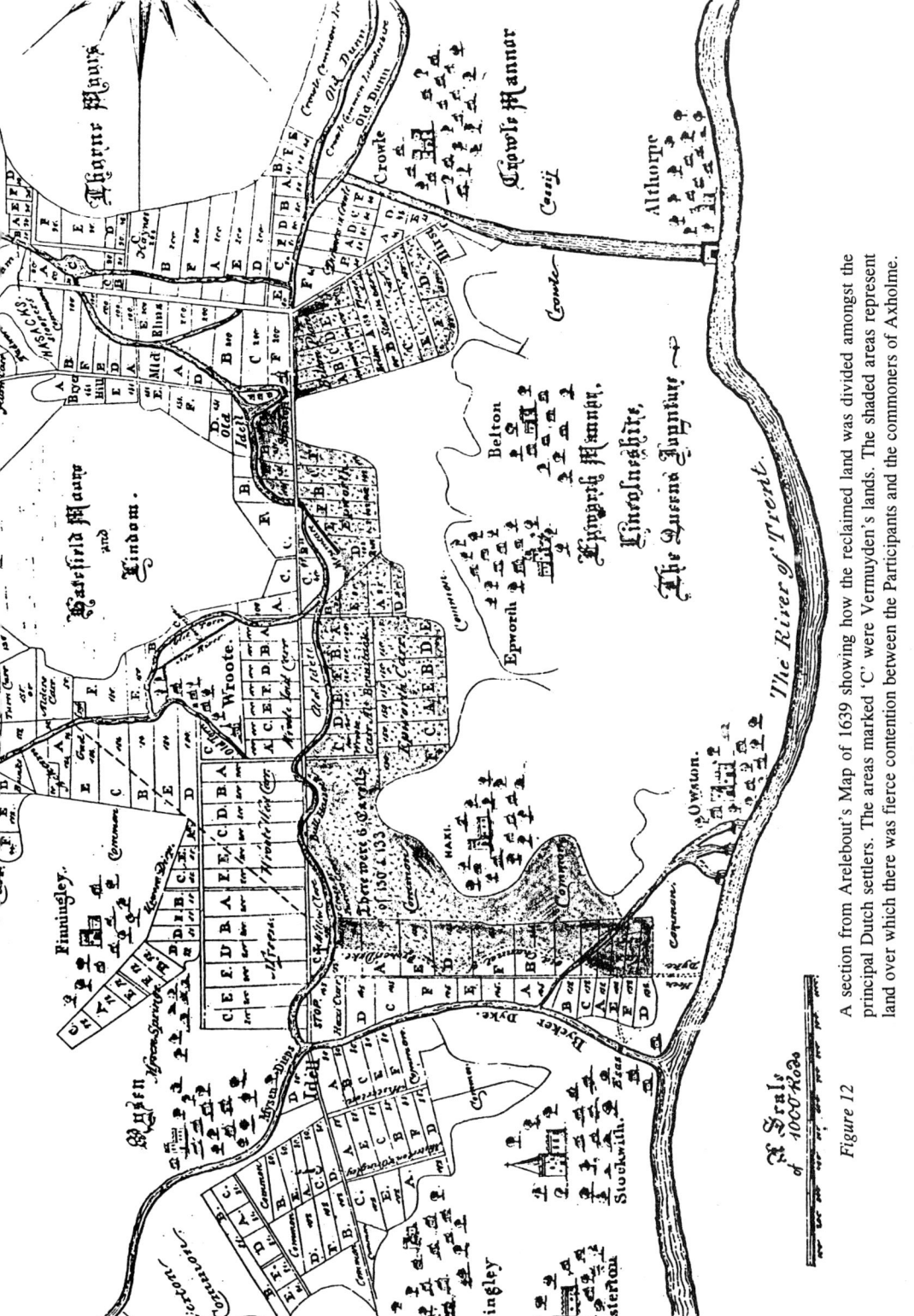

*Figure 12*

A section from Arelebout's Map of 1639 showing how the reclaimed land was divided amongst the principal Dutch settlers. The areas marked 'C' were Vermuyden's lands. The shaded areas represent land over which there was fierce contention between the Participants and the commoners of Axholme.

*Lister'* cover the early years of the constant protest against the drainage, the former dealing with Vermuyden's time and the latter being set in the Civil War. Although somewhat lurid and fanciful both these novels nevertheless make interesting attempts to include highly probable events.

Axholme's Commoners raised two companies of foot soldiers (495 men) for the Ironsides and the settlers provided a Royalist Troop of Cavalry. Isle men spread a rumour that Axholme was under imminent attack from the south and under this guise they reaped havoc in that area destroying flood gates on the Snow Sewer as well as the sluice at Misterton Soss. Many houses were destroyed and some 4,000 acres inundated. The Sheriff of Lincoln had the sluices repaired only to see a rabble force of some 400 villagers promptly ruin them again.

John Lilburne, a colourful Lieutenant Colonel who had served with the Roundheads, and who was often in trouble for his outspoken views, was persuaded by Daniel Noddel, solicitor for the Commoners, to take up their cause. He was joined by Major John Wildman and the Epworth commoners were delighted with the support of these two officers.

Action was not long in coming for when in 1650, the Participants won a legal action against the Commoners it was simply ignored and the Isle men (with military assistance) made a ferocious attack on the Sandtoft stockade, destroying some fifty buildings as well as crops on the disputed land. Some land was seized and in the shareout, Lilburne and Wildman were allocated 2,000 acres. (REF.4)

The battles in court for the right to farm the lands in question went on year after year. The Participants continued to seek redress for damage to their fields and property and in 1653 a ruling in their favour wanted the guilty parties arrested and punished. Noddel asked for proceedings to be delayed whilst there was so much unrest and in the meantime the Participants lost more and more of their allocated land.

When the turncoat, Nathaniel Reading was appointed as Collector of Taxes for the settlers in 1655, many of the Commoners of Epworth refused to pay, so he impounded their cattle in the pinfold at Hatfield. A party of Axholme men invaded that village; rescued their cattle and almost killed Thomas Heddon (the Hatfield constable) in the process.

General Whalley was sent to negotiate a settlement, but the Commoners showed scant respect for his intervention declaring that if Cromwell himself had been sent they would make no more of him than an ordinary person. However, with reinforcements Whalley did bring the rioters to book and in December 1655, some fifty of them faced trial before the Court of Sewers. Many of these were Epworth men and they were fined in various sums.

There was calm for a few months before squabbles flared afresh and in just five years Reading's men were involved in over thirty skirmishes with the Isleonians, most of which were against the men of Epworth, Misterton and Gringley. A 78 year old witness at a suit brought by the Gentlemen of Epworth against the

Participants in 1685, claimed that the drainage work had not improved the land and said that the land taken by Vermuyden had been the best land before the drainage.

Rioting occurred again in 1688 when yet another onslaught on Sandtoft took place with its church, buildings and machinery destroyed. An agreement between the two sides brought some respite in 1691 until Reading claimed £3,000 in rent arrears. In retaliation a mob (led by a Mrs Popplewell) destroyed Reading's barns, cattle and crops and when his house was fired, he was fortunate to escape. He was paid £600 in damages, but wished for no further action to be brought against the rioters.(REF.5)

Turncoat that he may have been, Reading worked to bring peace and after 1691 the rioting declined considerably. There were still some disturbances and the military were encamped on Lieutenant Colonel Robert Reading's farm at Sandtoft in 1714, to prevent damage to land and stock. We find this son of Nathaniel Reading defending a final lawsuit brought by the commoners in 1719.

In reality there were no winners from this almost century long conflict. The Participants failed in their agricultural enterprise and could not meet their debts to their backers and in time most of the original settlers had returned home - poor and disappointed. Their successors battled on with the succeeding generations of disgruntled Isleonians, a situation that did little to ensure positive progress in agriculture.

REFERENCES
1. Cory, V.        *Hatfield and Axholme. An Historical Review.*
                  Providence Press, 1985.
2. Thirsk, J.     *The Isle of Axholme before Vermuyden.*
                  Agricultural History Review. Vol.1, 1953.
3. Stonehouse,W.B. (1839) op.cit.
4. Cory,V.        (1985) op.cit.
5. Read, W.       (1858) op.cit.

A commercial postcard of the Market Cross as it looked before the second World War.
*Courtesy of Miss Marjorie Trimingham.*

John Wesley had this picture of his home in flames engraved as an emblem under one of his portraits, and it is reproduced here from the original vignette.*

*Its motto had the well known words 'is not this a brand plucked out of the burning?' where Wesley refers to his own dramatic rescue.

*Reproduced from Stonehouse's History and Topography of the Isle of Axholme.*

Epworth Rectory - the home of the Wesley Family. This photograph shows the house around the middle of this century prior to the removal of the extension to the left. *Courtesy of Edwin Harrison*

# CHAPTER FIVE

## The Wesley Family

Epworth is synonymous with Methodism and the world renowned founder of that mighty church, John Wesley was born in the town. Book after book has been written about the Methodist leader and they still continue to be published at quite frequent intervals! The lives of his parents and brothers have also been fairly well covered in various books, but the seven Wesley daughters have never received much attention. An American author wrote about the girls in 1988 and the writer's own account of their lives can be seen in the Local History collection at Doncaster Public Library. I do not feel that long accounts of this famous family are appropriate in this work, but no examination of Epworth's history should neglect the hearth and home of the town's most famous son.

Both Samuel Wesley and his wife Susanna, came from distinguished families dating back to the pre-conquest times, the former having forebears who fought in the Crusades and the latter descending from ancestry pre-dating William the Conqueror. They had much in common before they ever met, for both had clergyman fathers who were driven from their livings by the Act of Uniformity. It is therefore something of a surprise that this couple, coming from such a strong puritan background, should have spurned dissent and chose to devote themselves to the Anglican cause.

Doctor Annesley, Susanna's father, often invited clerics to his home in Spital's Yard, London, to hold discussions and debates, and this was where Samuel met his wife to be. He was quickly attracted to the slim and extremely beautiful young lady and it was not long before they were married in 1689 (when the bride was just 19 and the groom 27). Ordained by this time, Samuel's first appointment was to serve as Chaplain on a man-o-war, but marriage made him leave the sea to take up a curacy in Holborn, London. Their first child, Samuel was born here, one of a number of difficult births that Susanna had to endure.

Early in 1691 the family moved to the secluded hamlet of South Ormsby in Lincolnshire where Samuel was the incumbent at St Leonard's Church. In her first seven years of marriage Susanna had seven children, but three of these died early in life and were buried at South Ormsby and so it was a family of six who moved into Epworth Rectory in 1697. Hetty, their eighth child was born that year, but the next five years saw a string of infant deaths and it must have been a very relieved mother who saw Anne Wesley come into the world in 1702 and go on to survive. By 1709 the family was complete, with the births of John (1703), Martha (1706), Charles (1707) and Kezziah in 1709. A boy, born in 1705, was accidentally smothered by the nurse.

Susanna Wesley is of course renowned the world over for the way in which she trained and educated all ten of her sons and daughters at the Epworth Rectory, a

*Figure Thirteen*
  Part of a letter from John Wesley to William Wilberforce, 1790 and written when he was 87 years old.

business that covered some twenty years or more. It was a strict and rigorous schooling and the devoted mother exercised a remarkable talent and patience across her family's formative years. Her children were put through a meticulously controlled regime by which they received instruction in mental, moral, educational and spiritual aspects as well as in habits of dressing, sleeping, eating, hygiene and personal conduct.

Epworth's 'first lady' carried out all this industry in living with a husband who was hopeless at managing the family business so this was also frequently left in Susanna's capable hands. On her own admission she rarely saw eye to eye with her spouse and arguments were almost a daily occurrence. The fierce little academic was undoubtedly a fine scholar and something of a city man, but certainly no farmer and his efforts at husbandry were often the joke of the parish.

The totally destructive fire of 1709 in which the young John Wesley almost perished, split up the family for a time, but it was only a year later that Samuel, with the help of the Ecclesiastical Commissioners built a substantial new, brick Rectory. As before, it was only ever half furnished and there were times when the family lived on bread and water, but they had a home again. To trouble them more they suffered the mysterious hauntings of 1716/17, although there are those who feel they may have been the work of local mischief makers.

We leave Samuel and Susanna to take a brief look in turn, at each of their children. The eldest of the Wesley brothers, Samuel, received some of his early education at John Holland's Academy in Epworth. He later attended Westminster School and Oxford; took Holy Orders and returned to Westminster School as a teacher. Later still, now married, he was appointed to the Headship of Blundell's School at Tiverton in Devon, where he remained until his death at the age of 49 in 1739. Samuel Wesley, junior, is remembered as a scholar, excellent teacher, High Anglican, Jacobite, poet and satirist. His epitaph sets the seal on his life, 'an excellent preacher....whose best sermon was the constant example of an edifying life'.

Were it not for John Wesley we would not be able to tell of his family or of Methodism or its fame at Epworth. Like his brothers, he too excelled at public school and university and entered the Church. The facts of his life are so well known especially about his work that we will concentrate more upon his character, and what a character, for it has been said of him that he did the work of four men in what he achieved in his long lifetime.

John Wesley was a superb organiser and had his finger on every aspect of the Methodist movement. Neat and meticulous in his appearance and hygiene he wanted the same conscientious application in his class leaders, exhorters, local and travelling preachers. Wesley would preach two to four times a day every day and he would stick to delivering his 5am sermon all his life. He travelled a quarter of a million miles, mostly on horseback and preached over 40,000 sermons. He often exercised his literary skill whilst in the saddle and perhaps he

*TABLE TWO*

## THE EPWORTH WESLEY FAMILY (REF.1)

| Name | Birthplace | Born | Died | Burial Place | Age |
|---|---|---|---|---|---|
| Samuel Wesley,S(REF.2) | Whitchurch | late 1662 | 4/25/1735 | Epworth Churchyard | 73 |
| Susanna Wesley | London | 1/20/1669 | 7/23/1742 | Bunhill Fields, London | 73 |
| **CHILDREN** | | | | | |
| 1. Samuel Jr | London | 2/10/1690 | 11/6/1739 | Tiverton | 49 |
| 2. Susanna | South Ormsby | 1691 | 4/1693 | South Ormsby | Infant |
| 3. Emilia (Harper) | " " | 1/1692 | 1771 | London | 79 |
| 4. Annesley | | | | | |
| 5. Jedediah twins | " " | 1694 | 1/31/1695 | South Ormsby | Infants |
| 6. Sussanna (Ellison) | " " | 1695 | 12/7/1764 | London | 69 |
| 7. Mary (Whitelamb)(REF.3) | " | 1696 | 11/1734 | Wroote | 38 |
| 8. Mehetabel (Wright) | Epworth | 1697 | 3/21/1750 | London | 53 |
| 9. Not known whether boy or girl | " | 1698 | soon died | Epworth | Infant |
| 10. John | Epworth | 5/18/1699 | soon died | Epworth | Infant |
| 11. Benjamin | " | 1700 | " | " | " |
| 12. & 13. Unnamed twins | " | 5/17/1701 | " | " | " |
| 14. Anne (Lambert) | " | 1702 | ? | ? | ? |
| 15. John | " | 6/17/1703 | 3/2/1791 | City Road, London | 87 |
| 16. Son smothered by nurse | " | 5/8/1705 | 5/30/05 | Epworth | Infant |
| 17. Martha (Hall) | " | 5/8/1706 | 7/19/1791 | City Road, London | 85 |
| 18. Charles | " | 12/18/1707 | 3/29/1788 | Marylebone, London | 80 |
| 19. Kezziah | " | 3/1709 | 3/9/1741 | London | 32 |

REFERENCES
1. Data assembled chiefly from Stevenson's Memorials of the Wesley Family and Adam Clarke's Memoirs of the Wesley Family.
2. Stevenson gives 12/17/1662 as Samuel Wesley's birth date, but according to Kirk, the Parish register of Whitchurch gives 12/17/1662 as the date of his baptism.
3. Stevenson lists Mary Wesley's place of birth as Epworth in 1696, but Dr Frank Baker's more recent research establishes 1697 as the date of arrival of the Wesley's at Epworth, so Mary must have been born at South Ormsby.

Samuel and Susanna Wesley from original portraits by Richard Douglas by courtesy of the Epworth Old Rectory. They had 19 children, 10 of whom died at a very early age.

John and Charles Wesley in their late thirties from orginal portraits by Richard Douglas. *Courtesy Epworth Old Rectory*

needed to, for he wrote close on three hundred books and pamphlets on numerous aspects of divinity and theology as well as on music, natural history, poetry, science, medicine and the metaphysical, moral and political branches of philosophy. It was said of him that he was the best gatherer and scatterer of useful knowledge of his century.

John Wesley, however, was never successful in his relationships with the ladies. His early fancy for Kitty Hargreaves came to nothing and he asked Grace Murray to marry him when she was already engaged to one of his preachers. He asked his mother for advice in regard to his liking for Betty Kirkham and when he did at last get himself married to Molly Vazeille in 1751, it was a disaster from the start. She would not travel around the country with him and he would not change his way of life. She tried to smear his character and deserted him in January 1758, and after that they had only a correspondence marriage. Molly died in 1781 leaving her husband only her wedding ring.

A failure in marriage or not, John Wesley has to be admired for all the strengths of his personality and disposition. He adored the countryside, loved children and worked ceaselessly as a social pioneer. He provided Sunday Schools, Day Schools and Charity Schools; founded orphanages and homes for the elderly; established a Preachers' Fund, tried to abolish the slave trade and to reform the prisons. To trace all the qualities of such a man is an impossible task. Of course he did have his faults, but they are far, far outweighed by his virtues. He is remembered in particular for his wonderful Journal and one of his sayings which he certainly lived out reads:

> *'Do all the good you can,*
> *By all the means you can,*
> *In all the ways you can,*
> *In all the places you can,*
> *At all the times you can,*
> *To all the people you can,*
> *As long as ever you can.'*

Charles Wesley too was an accomplished scholar, theologian and evangelist and perhaps the most likeable member of the Wesley family. He was very popular at Westminster School; a witty intellectual, sportsman, and Captain of the school in 1725. He missioned in South Georgia with John in 1735, but after his conversion in 1738 accepted a curacy at Islington. He was soon sacked, as the Vicar did not want his evangelistic style so Charles took to the road with his brother as a travelling evangelist.

Charles married Sarah Gwynne, the daughter of a wealthy Welsh magistrate, in 1749. Their two sons, Samuel and Charles, both became very talented musicians and were excellent organists. We are indebted to Charles' daughter Sally for much of our knowledge of the Wesley family, for it was she who passed much information in this respect to Adam Clarke, an early biographer. Charles gave up horseback evangelism in 1756 and settled to work in Bristol. There he was instrumental in helping to establish a strong Methodist cause. In 1771 the family moved to Marylebone in London where Charles was a frequent visitor to the prisoners in Newgate and he even wrote a book of hymns especially for them. It is as the great Methodist hymnologist that Charles is supremely remembered for the theology of his several thousand hymns remains unsurpassed.

It has been said that the seven Wesley girls faced all the different kinds of frustration, heartache, poverty, despair, happiness, triumph and defeat characteristic of the T.V. soap operas of today. All the girls were of fine appearance, but their temperaments varied considerably. They received a good, sound, home education, but higher learning was out of question in those days and their parents simply wanted to see them find suitable partners in marriage. Many of the visitors to the Rectory were rough and ready local tradesman and they were not considered suitable for these cultured young ladies. Their father appears to have lacked much sympathy or understanding in regard to the various love affairs in which the girls indulged and both he and his sons frequently interfered and criticised them to an unfeeling and sometimes inconsiderate degree.

Emilia, usually called Emmy in the family, was the eldest daughter and often took the part of her mother in looking after her younger sisters. Indeed, she may have been put on in this respect, for she certainly longed to escape from the drudgery of both Epworth and Wroot. After a longish affair with Robert Leybourne, whom she had met in London, Emilia spent some time as a governess in Lincoln. Here at Miss Taylor's Boarding School, she was overworked and underpaid, and so she left to set up her own school in Gainsborough.

Another love affair in her early forties ended in disaster mainly because of criticism from her brother John. Emilia came back to Epworth to nurse her dying father who passed away in 1735. It was perhaps a pity that she did not become Robert Leybourne's wife, for he went on to achieve high academic standing and was very successful in the Anglican Church. As it happened, when she was 43 years of age, Emilia married Robert Harper, an Epworth apothecary, who spent all her money and treated her most shamefully. Eventually he left her and emigrated to America, leaving Emilia to look after an ailing daughter, who died soon afterwards.

John Wesley provided a home for Emilia in London's West Street adjacent to his London Headquarters and here she remained for 25 years until her death in 1771 at the age of 79. She proved a great help to her brother in London and long before the Deaconess Order was thought of, she performed that role as she ministered to the sick and suffering at the Foundery. It seems she had not seen the last of the Epworth Rectory ghost, for Emilia claimed that 'Old Jeffrey' had visited her on several occasions in West Street.

The second daughter, Susanna Wesley, made a hasty and regrettable marriage in 1721 whilst on a visit to her uncle Matthew in London. Her unfortunate choice was Richard Ellison, a gentleman farmer of a vulgar and coarse nature. They had four children in what was a nasty and violent relationship, for Ellison frequently thrashed Susanna in the most cruel manner, at times coming near to killing her. When their London home was destroyed by fire Susanna took the opportunity to escape from her husband. She never lived with him again although the wily rogue even had his own death announced in a newspaper, to entice Susanna to Lincolnshire, where he was then living. She fell for the ruse and came north for the funeral, but on finding Richard very much alive, she quickly beat a hasty retreat back to London.

The short life of Mary (Molly) Wesley was ended by her untimely death in 1734, after just one year of wedded bliss. It had seemed as if the gentle, quiet and serene, but crippled Molly would never marry but her chance came along when her parents took in Johnny Whitelamb, a local lad from Wroot. Eventually they put Johnny through Oxford and he took Holy Orders. Samuel Wesley arranged for him to take over the living at Wroot's St Pancras Church. Here in that church, he may have buried his wife and new born child, for a plaque on its north wall records the interment of Samuel Smyth, but below this inscription it continues 'Also Mary Whitelamb, wife of the late Rector of Wroot'.

Hetty Wesley (Mehetabel), the beautiful, bouncy, flamboyant tearaway of Samuel's seven daughters, is by far the most well known. At the age of eight she could read the New Testament - in Greek! Her parents were frustrated by her many infatuations and love affairs and she was sent off to serve as a governess with the Grantham family at Kelstern, near Louth. Here she continued a clandestine love affair and when her father would not allow her to marry, she eloped with her lawyer friend to Lincoln. There something quickly went seriously amiss for after just one night of passion, Hetty returned home to Epworth in disgrace ! Her father was furious and later on, learning that she was pregnant, forced her into a marriage with William Wright, an illiterate plumber from Louth.

Hetty's life thereafter was a tale of unhappiness and grief, as child after child was born, quickly to die. The Wrights set up business in London's Soho district, and there, after more than 20 years of distress and worry (mostly brought on by her father's unforgiving attitude), Hetty died in 1750 at the age of 53.

Anne Wesley married John Lambert (an Epworth land surveyor) at Finningley, on 2nd December,1725. Before her marriage she is thought to have worked at Thorne as a governess, but returned home when her mistress took ill. She is unique amongst the Wesley girls for she seems to have been the only one to have enjoyed a happy life. The Lamberts eventually settled at Hatfield in Hertfordshire and are known to have had a son whom they christened, John.

Martha Wesley was the sobersides of the family, but had the most charming and engaging personality. She courted many men whilst still young; John Romley, the Wroot Schoolmaster and curate, several lovers at Kelstern where she worked at the same house as Hetty, but as a companion helper; Matthew Horberry, a Lincoln College graduate and Benjamin Ingham, a member of the Holy Club at Oxford.

Then she met the Rev Westley Hall at her uncle's home in London. They were engaged, but this did not stop her fiancé, a notorious womaniser, from proposing marriage to Martha's younger sister, Kezziah, whilst on a visit to Epworth. He later forgot Kezziah and married Martha on 13th September,1735. There is perhaps some significance in the fact that two Wesley girls married just a few months after their father's death, probably feeling something of a release from the overbearing and dictatorial influence of the Rector's regime.

Westley Hall could never curb his love of women and he was constantly unfaithful to Martha, yet she stuck by him through it all even bringing up one of her husband's offspring by one of his mistresses. Their ten children all died in infancy, excepting for a boy who survived until he was 14, but only because he was cared for by John and Charles Wesley. Hall eventually deserted Martha and went to the West Indies, with yet another mistress ! Years later he returned to England, but it is uncertain as to whether he was reconciled to Martha, although she cared for him until his death in 1776. Martha herself outlived all her brothers and sisters and was laid to rest in the same vault as the Methodist leader in London's City Road Chapel in 1791. An inscription on the tomb states, 'She opened her mouth with wisdom and in her tongue was the law of kindness'.

Kezziah, the last of the Wesley girls was never very robust, however she had ambition, but repeated illness and her inferiority complex prevented her progress. She worked as a pupil teacher with her sister Emilia in the Boarding School at Lincoln, but was not successful. Receiving only board and lodging, she complained that she could not keep up a proper appearance, but her shy and retreating disposition did not help matters and so she returned home. Her jilting by Westley Hall shattered her and she never really recovered from the trauma. Her dejection and despair may have caused her addiction to snuff, a habit which her brother Charles tried to persuade her to break off.

When her mother had to vacate the Epworth Rectory in 1736, Kezziah lived at Tiverton with her eldest brother and also spent some time with the Halls and the Gambolds before settling in as a boarding guest at the home of Henry Piers, the Vicar of Bexley. Whilst there she courted an unknown suitor and became engaged, but her death on 10th March,1741 (when she was only 32 ) robbed her of marriage.

In some ways the Wesley girls remind us of the Bronte sisters of Howarth as both families lived in country parsonages, which, although in different times and terrain were both remote and desolate areas. Unlike the talented Brontes however, the Wesley girls (with the possible exception of Hetty) had no literary genius to enlighten their gloom to provide imaginative escapism. Once they were into adolescence their way ahead was unsure and frustrating and their anxious parents could only wait and see how their daughters would make out in regard to careers and marriages.

SOME USEFUL BOOKS ABOUT THE WESLEY FAMILY

1. Clarke, Adam *Memoirs of the Wesley Family*. W.Tegg, London, 1836.
2. Tyerman, L. *Life and Times of the Reverend Samuel Wesley - Rector of Epworth*. Simpkin, Marshall & Co Ltd, London, 1866.
3. Tyerman, L. *Life and Times of John Wesley, M.A.* Harper Bros., New York, 1872.
4. Edwards, Maldwyn *Family Circle. A Study of the Epworth Household in relation to John and Charles Wesley*. Epworth Press, 1949.
5. Harmon, Rebecca *Susanna, Mother of the Wesleys*. Hodder & Stoughton, 1968.
6. Maser, F.E. *Seven Sisters in Search of Love*. Academy Books. USA, 1988.
7. Wesley, John. *The Journal. Nehemiah Curnock 'Ed.* 8 vols. Epworth Press, 1938.

John Wesley preaching from his father's grave in Epworth Churchyard. *Reproduced from 'Epworth - What to See and How to Get There. A Lancashire & Yorkshire Railway booklet 1905, courtesy of Miss Marjorie Trimingham.*

The grave of Rev Samuel Wesley. It has undergone at least two restorations and part of the inscription reads: 'As he lived, so he died, In the true Catholic Faith, Of the Holy Trinity in Unity. And that Jesus Christ in God Incarnate. And the only Saviour of Mankind.'

An earlier view of the former Anglican Mission Church which was built to cater for worshippers living in Epworth's western approaches. It was opened in 1886. *Courtesy of Edwin Harrison.*

# CHAPTER SIX

## Church and Chapel

The Doomsday Book gives the suggestion of established Christianity in Axholme by its reference to a church existing at Crowle and it is likely that Epworth itself knew Christian worship at this early period. In the midst of the battles of the warring Saxon monarchs, and the later ravages of the Danes, the Christian message was sown and was to spring to life under the Norman enthusiasm for building churches and monasteries.

The Norman Barons in Axholme quickly provided churches at Haxey, Owston, Belton and Epworth. Fourteen Rectors of Epworth's St Andrews Church were presented to their livings by the Prior and Convent of Newburgh during the 14th and 15th centuries, but the architecture of this church suggests that it dates from as early as the 12th century.

In those days St Andrews was 'Catholic' until the establishment of the Church of England with the English Sovereign as its head. The little village of Epworth would see the effect of Henry VIII's savage suppression of monasticism in the seizure of nearby Low Melwood Priory and the confiscation of its funds, lands and valuables. Most of the monks of that establishment fared better than many, for they all received quite handsome pensions.

St Andrew's had two chantries as early as 1344, one of which was for John de Mowbray. Its priests were very poorly paid and folk made fun of their poor apparel. In 1365 the staff was reduced to a warden who was paid 50 shillings a year and two clerks who received 30 shillings a year, plus food and clothing. By then it seems they were fitted out with new and more appropriate vestments.(REF.1). Stonehouse lists thirteen presentations to these chantries between the years 1347 and 1501.(REF.2)

The sense of bygone centuries of worship is very strong as you walk up the ancient stone-flagged Church Walk to the church's entrance. The centre portion of St Andrew's has a 12th century association, although what we see today are three strains of architecture; Early English, Decorated and Perpendicular.

The Chancel arch, aisle arcades and the responds at the eastern end are all of the Early English period of 1189 to 1272. Typical of the Decorated period are the two-light windows in the west-end of the north aisle (used as a choir vestry) and also the chancel's three-light south windows with their reticulated tracery.

The predominating style is Perpendicular (1377 to 1547) and is seen in all the exterior, except the tall chancel. The tower (now without its earlier pinnacles) also belongs to this period as does the priest's vestry with its heavy oak doorway; the south and north aisles, the clerestory and the west and north embattled chapels. The chancel was partly destroyed in 1642 and later the side chapels were demolished and then the chancel was redesigned in the 1670's. There were

*Table Three*
## LIST OF RECTORS AT ST ANDREW'S CHURCH, EPWORTH AS FAR AS CAN BE ASCERTAINED

|  |  |  |  |
|---|---|---|---|
|  | William de Noot | 1735 | Samuel Hirst |
| 1319 | William Wigne | 1746 | John Hay |
| 1320 | William Thetilthorpe | 1751 | Thomas Lowe |
| 1322 | William de Clyne | 1757 | William Anderson |
| 1354 | William Naresby | 1784 | George Anderson |
| 1360 | Joannes de Denton | 1785 | John Robinson |
| 1365 | William Galby | 1801 | John Marshall |
|  | Richard Trevet | 1802 | James Hook |
| 1422 | Robert Blacklow | 1804 | Caley Illingworth |
| 1422 | Nicholas Bowey | 1823 | George Beckett |
|  | John Stowd | 1843 | Charles Dundas |
| 1463 | William Sheffield | 1883 | Henry Overton |
| 1482 | Richard Brandholme | 1897 | Neville Dundas |
| 1488 | Christopher Lofthouse | 1899 | James Greaves |
| 1500 | John Laton | 1926 | William Arthur Gough |
| 1508 | Thomas Barker | 1930 | Cosby Hudlestone Stokes |
| 1518 | Thomas Thorpe | 1933 | Osbert Morduant Burrows |
|  | Robertus Metcalfe | 1951 | Mervyn Armstrong |
| *(Registers defective until 1641)* | | 1955 | William Benjamin Harvey |
| 1641 | Robert Gale | 1981 | Arthur Makel |
| 1696 | Samuel Wesley | 1994 | Derek Brown |

## LIST OF MINISTERS AT THE WESLEY MEMORIAL METHODIST CHURCH

| | | | | | |
|---|---|---|---|---|---|
| 1889/91 | Robert Lickes | 1913/17 | W.Allen Phillips | 1938/42 | W.M.P.Wilkes |
| 1891/94 | Henry Parkes | 1917/18 | John. S. Elmont | 1942/46 | S.H.Bullough |
| 1894/97 | Henry. R. Burton | 1918/19 | William Taggart | 1946/51 | C.P.Bardsley |
| 1897/98 | Samuel Sheard | 1919/21 | J.Warren Milward | 1951/54 | J. Goldsbrough |
| 1898/00 | Joseph.B.Alger | 1921/24 | John Keddie | 1954/58 | W. le Cato Edwards |
| 1900/03 | Samuel Adcock | 1924/27 | J.R.Ellis | 1958/64 | George B. Fish |
| 1903/04 | S. Birt Coley | 1927/28 | H.C. Sidnall | 1964/70 | Thomas Russell |
| 1904/07 | F.H.Naylor | 1928/31 | J.W.Marsden | 1970/76 | Fred Bond |
| 1907/10 | Geo.B.Glover | 1931/34 | S.F.Hubbard | 1976/81 | Thomas Soulsby |
| 1910/13 | Edward Jones | 1934/38 | J.G.Radford | 1981/86 | Paul Waterfield |
| | | | | 1986/94 | Gordon Gatward |
| | | | | 1994 | Norman Smith |

The old Communion plate of Epworth Parish Church once used by John and Charles Wesley, consisting of a flagon, paten, chalice and maser (alms bowl). The chalice is dated 1706.

*Reproduced from 'Epworth and its Surroundings', 1903.*

Epworth's Baptist Church pictured about 1900. It was built in 1857 at a cost of £300 and its schoolroom seen alongside was erected in 1881.

*Reproduced from 'Epworth and its Surroundings', 1903*

The Kilham Memorial chapel in Epworth's High Street seen at the turn of the century. Note its manse alongside *(left)* now serving as a Residential Home.

*Reproduced from 'Epworth and its Surroundings', 1903*

Members of the Methodist Church ready to depart on an outing to Matlock in the 1920's The coach Company, Scutts, are still in business. *Courtesy of Miss Marjorie Trimingham,* whose parents can be seen centrally in the foreground with Marjorie herself standing immediately to her father's right

A view from the gateway of the tiny Baptist Cemetery in Station Road from which some of the headstones inlaid in the wall can seen.

renovations to the north porch in 1721 and in 1817 to the south porch. Samuel Varley leaded the top of the tower in 1728 and Mr J.Varley leaded the nave roof in 1782.(REF 3)

There was considerable renovation in 1868 carried out by James Fowler of Louth, when both aisles were completely re-roofed and the nave floor was re-covered; choir seats were fitted and also a new pulpit and altar with altar railings. Some years later the old altar from this church was passed into the possession of the Wesley Memorial Church. The stained glass window in the chancel's east end was put in by the Church Needlework Society in 1878, in honour of the Rector, the Rev. Charles Dundas who died in 1883, having held the office for 39 years. His son filled a south side chancel window in memory of his father; Arthur Maw gave the beautiful windows in the north aisle in memory of various members of his family and more stained glass windows were given by the Needlework Society.(REF 4)

During the alterations, the entrance to a rood loft, which had been bricked up was re-discovered and opened out. A portion of the old 14th century rood screen was found and worked into the front of the priest's reading desk on the south side.(REF 5)

Numerous visitors to Epworth make for St Andrew's churchyard to view the grave of its best remembered incumbent, the Rev. Samuel Wesley, father of the world famous founder of Methodism. His resting place can be seen close to the south side of the church. He was the rector from 1696 until 1735 and is remembered as a firm, but fair shepherd of his flock. Epworth parish was a well paid living for those days, with a stipend of £200 per annum at a time when pluralities abounded, made inevitable by the very low stipends, meagre endowments and the lack of suitable residences. Seventy parishes in Lincolnshire then had no resident incumbent. Samuel Wesley incurred the wrath of his parishioners in 1705, when thinking that the church was in danger, he voted for the Tories. An angry mob ran-tanned the Rectory and four years later it may have been arsonists who burnt it down.

Holy Communion was very infrequent in 1744: 31 churches in Lincolnshire held it monthly, 239 held it quarterly and in 114 churches it was held just three times a year. Yet there were many confirmations in the County, no less than 5,000 in 1771 although Samuel Wesley complained that some of his Epworth flock had been confirmed twice and even three times ! (REF 6)

St Andrew's had a large choir in the 1730's, all males who all had their proper places with seats for the tenors, bases, trebles and counters of which there were 22,19, 12 and 12 again respectively. This choir of sixty five singers must have made an impressive sound and some of them were no doubt ancestors of present day families of the area; with names like Johnson, Maw, Coggan, Slingsby, Pashley, Fillingham and Pilsworth.

Richard Towris was one of the tenors and it is said his epitaph read:

*Figure Fourteen*

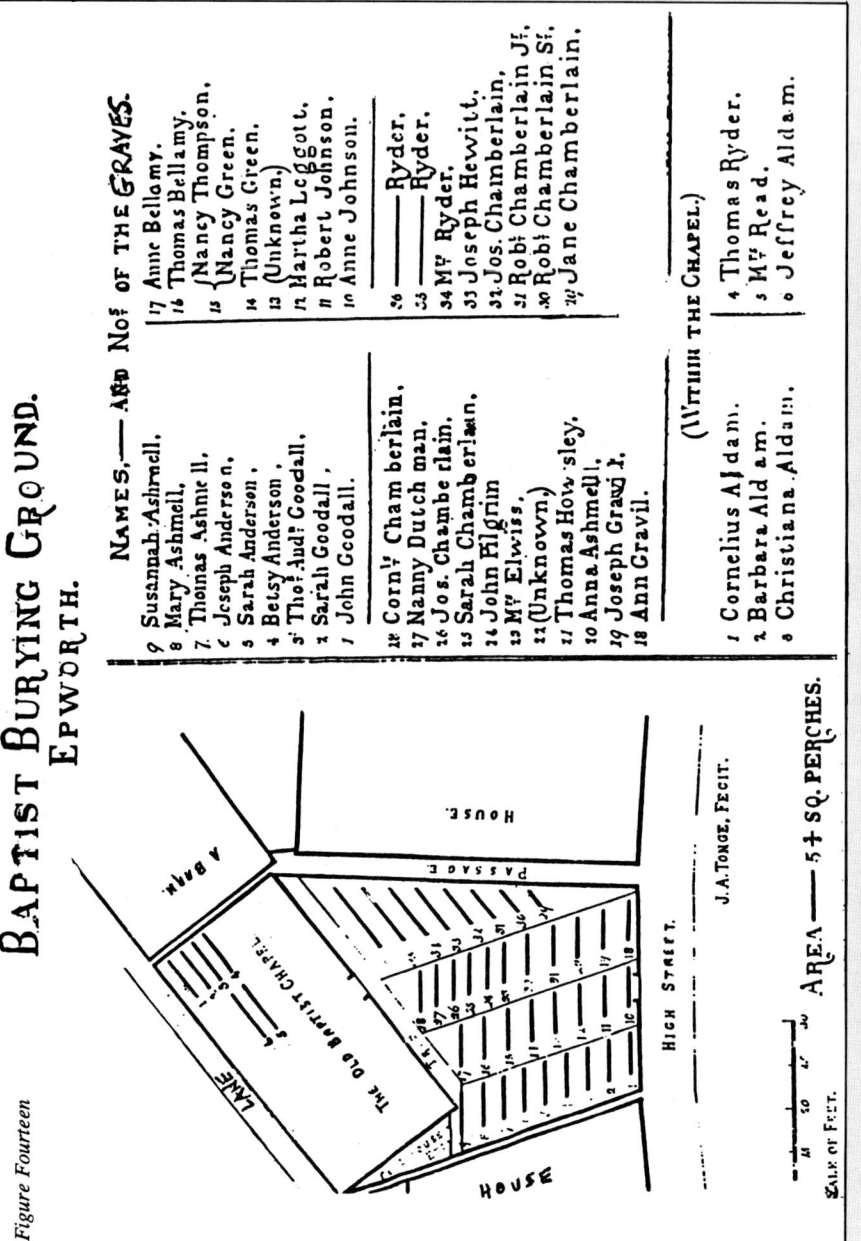

## PLAN OF FORMER BAPTIST CHAPEL AND GRAVEYARD IN STATION ROAD

The little graveyard can still be seen in Station Road, but what few gravestones remain are now inlaid at intervals inside the five perimeter walls. It is surprising to see how many people are buried here, and, as it seems as if some of the present headstones refer to people other than those listed, then many more may be interred here. *Reproduced from 'The Baptist Church, Epworth. Monumental and Memorial Inscriptions', compiled by Stephen R. Garner. Isle of Axholme Family History Circle, 1991.*

*'Who lies here? Who do you think?*
*Richard Towris and he liked drink*
*Drink ? Drink for why ?*
*Because Richard Towris was always dry?(REF 7)*

The Rev. Charles Dundas was a member of the first School Board of the Board School opened on the 9th October, 1876. Canon Overton, Rector from 1883 until 1897, was responsible for the building of the Mission Church in West End Road (now a private house). Its foundation stone was laid by Mrs Reeve of Leadenham House, a lady who had earlier spent some time in the Epworth Parish. Mr Belton Buttrick, a prominent Epworth resident who lived near to the new church, donated a stone which had been part of the Dutch/French Church at Sandtoft. It was cleaned up and inscribed with the words *'To the Glory of God. This stone from Sandtoft Church 1686, was laid as a Corner Stone of this Church. October 7th, 1886'*. At the time of writing it was covered with plaster, but the occupant of the 'Mission' tells me it may yet be uncovered to reveal its fame again.

The description of this church shows that even as a house it has not changed very much. It had a concrete foundation and bricks to the first floor line. Then it was continued upwards in wood, cement and plaster, topped off with a slated roof. Its spirelet and bellcot surmounted by a Latin Cross have gone. The chancel and nave measured just 44 feet by 17 feet and a small vestry was added to the west side. Heating was provided by a slow combustion 'tortoise' stove. Mr Henry Kelsey of Epworth was the building contractor and the Mission Church was officially opened by the Rev Canon Clements, sub Dean of Lincoln, on Sunday 23rd January, 1887.(REF 8)

The office of Church Warden, a position which has existed since the 12th century, was at one time the most important in regard to Parish Officers. Today they are involved principally in church affairs, but in Georgian and Victorian times they had a much wider brief in the community and served on various committees connected with the general running of the village or town. They looked after bridges, paths, tracks and roads and often personally made house to house collections to help disaster victims in other parts of the country. Such collections were known as briefs and they were used for all kinds of situations where relief was required and particularly for areas ravaged by fire or flood.

Church Warden's accounts often refer to beer having been provided for bell ringers; bells in earlier days playing a much more important part in parish life. They were rung for all sorts of reasons, such as for storm warnings and even celebrations of winning horse races and the 'common bell' was used to call the people together. An Epworth account of 8th July, 1789 read, *'Paid Glazer Isle. Parish Clerk half year's salary £2. 10s. 0d.'*

After Samuel Wesley's death a succession of Rectors did not even reside in the Epworth Parish, but put Curates in instead. The first of these was Thomas Gylby

Interior of the Kilham Memorial Church early this century. In January, 1897, a serious fire damaged the organ and the floor of the choir gallery fell in. The Church was closed for nine months but reopened on the 14th October the same year. *Courtesy of Miss Marjorie Trimingham*

The Thurlow Primitive Methodist Chapel built in 1883 - one of the many fine examples of Primitive Methodist Architecture. *Reproduced from 'Epworth and its Surroundings', 1903*

and it seems as if he may have appointed someone else (and a poor speller at that) to make the entries in the church register. A baptismal entry reads:
'*1736. June 18. Ann Douter of Alesander and An Clark.*'

During the 18th century the Parish Church had a regular collection for poor people at a monthly communion service and the money was initially given to the needy immediately after the service, but later on just at Christmas.

Samples of the amounts collected are as follows:

| Year | Average No. at Communion | Total amount collected |
|---|---|---|
| 1742 | 49 | 63s. 6d. |
| 1747 | 68 | 102s. 4d. |
| 1752 | 46 | 65s. 4d. |
| 1757 | 34 | 78s. 3d. |
| 1762 | 46 | 76s. 9d. |

It was reported in 1754 that the poor box always had a balance in hand (£3 that year) and possibly Epworth had less poverty in the 18th century than in the 19th. Typical entries from the poor box fund account are: May 8th,1750. '*Mr. Gervas was given the sum of £1. 12s. 0d for teaching reading to Zebediah Smewfield for 49 weeks, Marjorie and Solomon Waller for 40 weeks, and Edmund Foster for 40 to write.*' There was a similar entry every year as Thomas Gervas was the Master of the Free School and the rules allowed him to do some private tuition. Another entry reads, May 23rd, 1742. '*Took out of ye Poor Box 5s for ye cure of Thos Turner wife leg.*' (REF.9)

We leave the Anglican scene to consider the development of dissent and the movement that saw the Pilgrim Fathers sail to America may have had its origin in the Isle of Axholme. The Church Covenant of the Church Meeting at Epworth, Crowle and West Butterwick, dated 4th Jan, 1599 is signed by James Rayner, John Morton, William Brewster, William Bradford and Henry Helwise, plus 32 other signatories. Later Bradford and Brewster sailed to New England on the '*Mayflower*'. In all likelihood the Baptists (although not so called then) are the oldest non/conformists in Epworth and in those early days they were strongly opposed, but nevertheless they became well established in Axholme by the early 17th century and kept their rules very strictly.

A Baptist meeting at neighbouring West Butterwick on the 27th June, 1706, dismissed Isaac Ledsone because he had taken a wife 'contrary to the law of God' and had joined the Anglicans. A John Robson was also dismissed for his sin in resisting the advice of the Church. Again on the 5th November,1750 several members had gone over to the Methodists and were described as 'unfit for Christian communion with us!'

The Baptist Church register of 1673 gives 126 members spread over the groups at Epworth, Crowle and other Isle villages. Dippings (baptisms) were commonly held in the River Torne outside Dipping House Farm. (REF.10) A religious census of 1676 showed then that less than 5% of the people of Lincolnshire were

The Opening ceremony at the Primitive Methodist Sunday Schoolroom - 1909.
*Courtesy of Miss Majorie Trimingham*

This impressive Wesleyan Methodist Chapel used to stand in Chapel Street. It was built in 1821 at a cost of £900 and was used by the Wesleyan worshippers until the coming of the Wesley Memorial Church in High Street.   *Courtesy of Edwin Harrison*

nonconformists, but in Axholme they were relatively strong having 49 members at Owston Ferry, 57 at Epworth with 24 at Haxey. The figure giving the Baptist membership three years earlier suggests that this sect were in the majority as regards nonconformists. Axholme had established nonconformity long before the Toleration Act of 1689 and Belton was granted a licence for a Baptist Chapel in 1705.(REF.11) The present Baptist Chapel in Epworth was built in 1857 at a cost of £300 (the older one having to be pulled down) and a schoolroom was erected alongside in 1881.

There can be little doubt that Methodism came to Epworth early after John Wesley's conversion although the first chapels in the town may not have appeared until possibly the 1760's or later. Wesley himself made at least 36 visits to Epworth between 1742 and 1790. It is the diary entry for Saturday 26th June 1784 where we find his well known words, *'I rode to Epworth which I still love beyond most places in the world.'* In August 1788, Wesley complains about Mr Gibson at St Andrew's Church and says that because of his lack of piety he is reluctant to ask the Methodists to go there to hear him or have the sacrament administered by him.(REF.12)

Visiting Methodist travelling preachers were also in Epworth quite early, for in 1747 we find a Thomas Meyrick there, but it was not until 1765 that there was an official appointment of preachers. By the end of the 18th century there were forty Methodist chapels in Lincolnshire, but this figure rapidly increased to two hundred in the early decades of the 19th century.(REF.13)

James Barry was the Methodist Superintendent minister in 1781 when there was something of a revival amongst the young people working in the town's textile factories. They seem to have been a pretty wild and profligate group and Methodist visitors Thomas Saxton, Ann Toms and Ann Field went into the factories, but were met with some intimidation, so much so that they informed John Wesley about their experiences.

Wesley himself then ventured into this unruly scene and was instrumental in achieving a remarkable change. The lewdness and profaneness disappeared and one of the young converts was Alexander Kilham (the son of Simon Kilham, an Epworth weaver) who was to become the founder of the Methodist New Connexion, one of several breakaway movements from mainstream Methodism. Wesley accepted Kilham for the ministry in 1785, but in 1796 this second renowned son of Epworth was excluded from the Methodist Church, accused of outspokenness and defamation of Wesley's character. Many people sympathised with Kilham and his following very soon became a strong branch of Methodism and many villages in Axholme had a New Connexion chapel.

At first the Kilhamites shared the Wesleyan chapel, but this union was not a happy affair so they used a barn and also the Kilham home as places of worship. A Sunday School was held in Thomas Kilham's shop and there local tradesmen learned to read and write. At its simplest Kilham wanted to see laymen far more

Crowds at the Wesley Memorial Stone laying ceremony on 20th September, 1888. The first stone was laid by Rev C. Garrett, who as President of the Methodist Conference in 1882 had proposed the building of this Church as a public memorial to John and Charles Wesley.

*Courtesy of Miss Majorie Trimingham*

The attractive Wesley Memorial range of buildings with the Church, Manse and caretaker's house to the right. Pictured around 1900. *Reproduced from 'Epworth and its Surroundings', 1903*

involved in all aspects of Methodism.(REF.14) His ideas were before their time and as much as most of the reforms that Kilham advocated were later to become part of the Methodist Constitution, even today Methodist laymen do not have the privileges that he would like to have seen.

Kilham's fine work is commemorated today in the form of the impressive Kilham Memorial Chapel and School which was built in 1860. Built in red brick in Flemish bond with blue brick and limestone ashlar dressings, this former place of worship is still an attractive feature of Epworth's High Street. It was converted for use as a youth centre in the mid 1940's and has been used for that purpose ever since. The original ornate carved wooden pulpit and altar rails were taken to the Wesley Memorial Church opposite.

Another far more popular branch of Methodism came to Axholme from about 1819, when the Primitive Methodist Church spread like wild fire from its source at Mow Cop in Staffordshire. Its pioneers quickly spread their simple, but very effective gospel up through Leicestershire, Nottinghamshire and on throughout the Trent Valley. Chapels soon appeared in many parts of the Isle such as at Westwoodside in 1822, 1835 and 1861; at Luddington in 1841; Owston Ferry 1838; Epworth 1821; Eastoft 1820 and Crowle in 1842.

In 1883 the impressive Thurlow Primitive Methodist Chapel replaced an earlier one and in 1909 it opened its neighbouring Sunday School. This complex is now Wood's supermarket in Station Road. What we know as Wesleyan Methodism has been in Epworth for more than 250 years and is represented today by the world renowned Wesley Memorial Church. Prior to the opening of their church in 1889 the Wesleyans worshipped in the massive and solid Chapel Street premises. That building itself was rebuilt on the site of a previous chapel in 1821 at a cost of £900.

The Church in which Epworth's Methodists meet today was built on a site bought from Mr Blaydes in 1886 for £500 and its foundation stones were laid on 20th September, 1888, when it was estimated that 5,000 people visited the town on that day, the streets being gaily decorated and the church site itself *'was bright with flags'*. The building was officially opened on Thursday, 5th September, 1889, when the church was packed to capacity and an outdoor meeting was also necessary. By 1891, the attractive Manse and the caretaker's house were also in place. Prior to this the Superintendent minister had resided at Wesley House in Queen Street, which along with the chapel and school on either side of Pashley's Walk, was sold to Mr Blaydes in 1890.

The design of the Wesley Memorial Church is Victorian Gothic and the architect for the whole complex was Charles Bell. The walls of the church are of rock faced ashlar, except for the south side which is of yellow brick. There are ashlar dressings throughout and the roof is of Welsh slate. The square tower leads up to an octagonal stair turret and the belfry has louvred, double chamfered lancets topped with a spire having trefoiled lucarne windows. There is a fine entrance with its five stone steps leading up to the trefoil doorway with its double-chamfered arch.

Inside, the church has simple yet dignified iron columns supporting a very fine heavy timbered arch roof. The transept has a hammer beam roof and is airy and well lit, with a commanding stained glass window depicting the Commissioning of the Disciples, above which are life-sized profiles of John and Charles Wesley featured in a circular panel.

Other features include the communion table which was originally in the parish church and which was used by the Wesleys; the beautiful oak screen erected by the Needlework Society and unveiled in 1902; the carved oak font presented by Mrs Thomas Walker of Bolton and two more stained glass windows, one presented by Mrs Blaydes in memory of her husband and the other by Mr W.I.Breeze in memory of his wife, Emily.

It would be remiss of me not to mention another dearly loved little place of worship (a little off the beaten track) but dear to the hearts of the residents of Epworth's outlying Turbary. For years and years the folk of the Turbary improvised with one sort of building or another for worship and Mr and Mrs Frank Knowles were leading influences in ensuring that sooner or later a 'real' church would be built.

Mr John Trippett, a veteran local preacher, nicknamed the 'Methodist Bishop of the Turbary', was instrumental in starting a house church on the Turbary. He organised the villagers into subscribing for the purchase of a cottage to be used as a place of worship. The Knowles used their barn for the services and there were also socials, fun nights and concerts all held to raise funds for building the chapel. Bit by bit the money came in and the work started on the building of what we know today as the Turbary Mission. Mr S.Fox laid the first brick on Saturday 18th September,1926. Many other Turbary folk took a turn at laying a brick and things progressed rapidly, Miss Ishbel MacDonald carrying out the opening ceremony on Sunday 17th October,1926. The ceremonies continued on the following day when County Councillor Goodman of Rotherham said that it was the first time in the history of the Isle of Axholme that a daughter of a Prime Minister had opened a Mission church.(REF.15)

In the Census of Religious worship of 1851, St Andrew's Church had 138 people at the morning service whereas at the evening services at the Wesleyans, Primitive Methodists and Baptists there were congregations of 204, 250 and 60 respectively. The afternoon service at the Providence New Connexion was 120 and at West Carr 31.(REF.16) This shows that there were 803 worshippers which accounted for about half of the local population ! Today's churches in Epworth cannot match up to that record, but they are nevertheless vibrant and attractive elements of community life. The Wesley Memorial Church still enjoys a large Sunday morning congregation and the Baptists and Anglicans progress well, whilst the Turbary Mission still has occasional services. They all enjoy each other's company and often undertake united efforts.

REFERENCES
1.  Owen, Dorothy. M.  *Church and Society in Medieval Lincolnshire*. Lincolnshire Local History Society, 1971.
2.  Stonehouse, W.B.  (1839) op.cit.
3.  Messiter, A.F.  *Notes on Epworth Parish Life in the 18th century*. Elliot Stock, 1912.
4.  *Epworth and its Surroundings*.  Barnes and Breeze. 2nd Edition, 1903.
5.  Pevsner. Nicolaus and Harris. John. *The Buildings of England*. Lincolnshire. Penguin Books. 2nd Edition, 1989.
6.  Brears, C.  *Lincolnshire in the 17th and 18th Centuries*. A. Brown and Sons, Ltd., 1940.
7.  Messiter, A.F.  (1912) op.cit.
8.  *Epworth Bells Archive*.  January 1887. Mechanics' Institute Library, Epworth.
9.  Messiter, A.F.  (1912) op.cit.
10. Chesterman, A.& M.  *Axholme Baptists*. Isle of Axholme Printing Ltd.,1949
11. Brears, C.  (1940) op.cit.
12. Wesley, John.  *Journal of the Rev John Wesley*. Ed. N.Curnock. 8 Vols. Epworth Press, London, 1938.
13. Brears. C.  (1940) op. cit.
14. Groombridge. R.  *Life of Alexander Kilham*. Methodist New Connexion Publication, 1838.
15. *Epworth Bells Archive*.  (October 1926) op. cit.
16. *Ecclesiastical Census*.  1851.

The tiny chapel in Epworth Turbary - opened by Miss Ishbel MacDonald ( the daughter of the Prime Minister ) in 1926.

An early view of Station Road, Epworth looking towards the High Street and Tottermire Lane.
*Courtesy of Miss Marjorie Trimingham*

The restored pinfold in West End Road - an enclosure in which stray cattle used to be impounded and only released on payment of a fine. It was in the charge of a Parish officer known as a Pinder - sometimes called a Punder or Poundkeeper

# CHAPTER SEVEN

## Agriculture and Enclosure

During the Saxon and Norman periods most villages had the one or two large fields system of farming and these were divided into narrow strips of perhaps around a third of an acre which themselves were grouped into furlongs aligned to take advantage of the changing aspects of drainage and soil conditions throughout the field. Access to the individual selions was via a common baulk or headland.

In the later middle ages most land continued to be farmed in this open field system with the strips being shared by numerous tenants. All untilled land was common property on which cattle and fowls were kept and which often supplied villages with wood and peat. Some land was hedged in here and there, but in more than half of the villages, this system persisted well into the 18th century and in some cases much longer.

Staple crops of very early times were barley and wheat whilst later rye and hemp also became popular. The foreign settlers in Hatfield Chase and Axholme introduced tanning, weaving and spinning and these became significant industries, especially in the Epworth parish, but also in other Isle villages. The higher ground had been farmed for centuries and was little affected by the Drainage operations. During the reign of Charles I, hemp, barley and rye were grown in rotation in the Epworth Manor and on the demesne land, crops included barley, rye, wheat, oats, peas, beans and flax and there was also the pasture land. Barley took prime place and at that time accounted for a third of the arable land in use.(REF.1)

On the lower ground the farmers of Epworth were hard hit by the drainage scheme losing some 7,500 acres on the commons. Pastoral farmers cut down their stock numbers and tried to find alternative grazing. Drinking water was often in short supply in some parts, whilst flooding was a problem in others.

A significant contribution to the progress of agriculture in Axholme was the enormous activity and industry associated with the growing of hemp and flax. Epworth became noted for the skill of its people in the culture and successful preparation of various materials. The home made linen table-cloths were regarded as valuable possessions. Factory Lane in Doncaster (now no more) was so named because of a sacking factory set up there in 1769 by Mr Needham of Epworth.(REF.2) In the later years of the 18th century Epworth had four textile factories in operation engaged in spinning and weaving. It was said that nearly every barn in the town was stuffed with flax and there was work for many hands at £1 per week. Almost every house had its spinning wheel and the garments they made must have lasted well, for it was said that women wore gowns and cloaks used by their mothers. The dressing of flax and hemp was claimed to have been

*Figure Fifteen*

**OPEN FIELD FARMING - TYPICAL STRIP ARRANGEMENT**

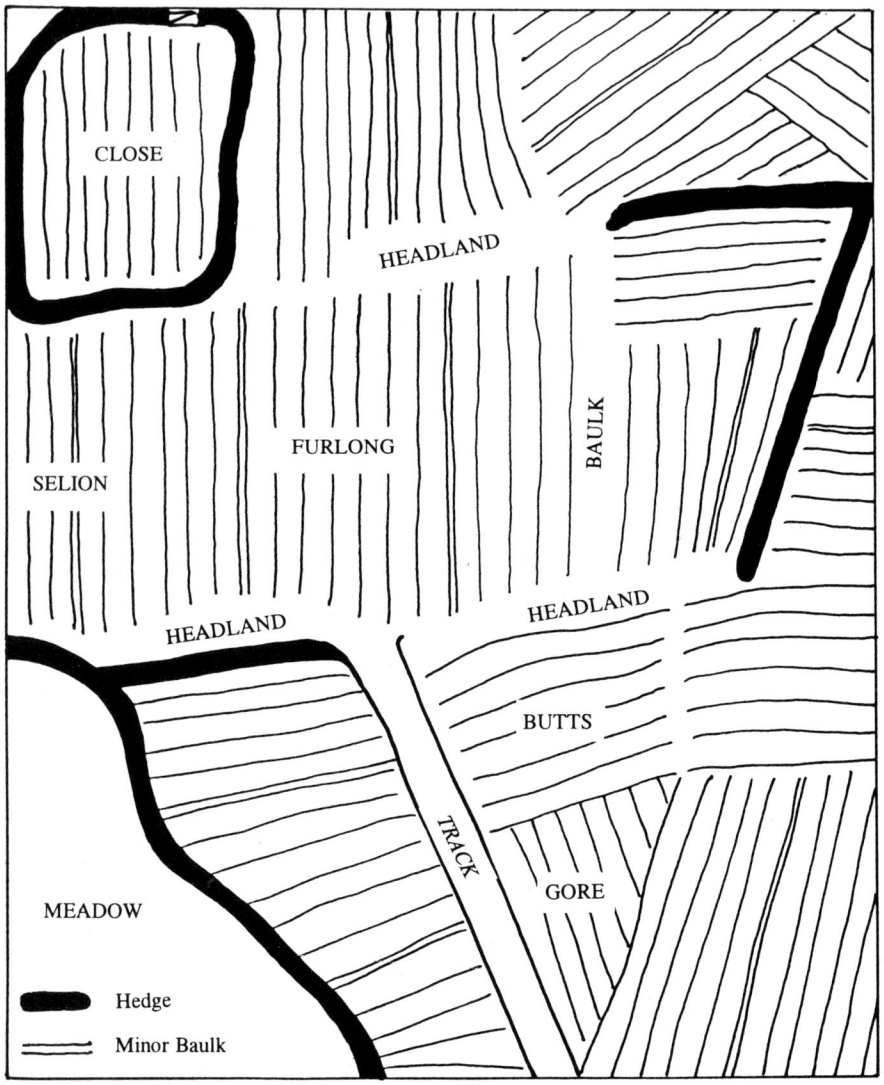

The Four large fields around Epworth were each grouped into 'furlongs' aligned so as to take advantage of the changing aspect of drainage and soil conditions throughout the field.
*Adapted from 'The Isle of Axholme - Man and Landscape' by permission Humberside Archaeology Unit.*

*Figure Sixteen*
**AN IMPRESSION OF STRIP FARMING IN THE EPWORTH AREA AS IT MAY HAVE APPEARED FOR SEVERAL CENTURIES EXTENDING INTO THE VICTORIAN PERIOD**

The open fields of the Epworth Parish beyond the top of Hollingsworth Lane and looking out over the Trent Valley

Epworth's principal industry in the 1850's.(REF.3) Rope, cordage, twine, sacking and canvas manufacturing were also common in Epworth and the Isle.

The growing of hemp and flax goes back to medieval times, the former providing the coarser fibres used in sacking and the latter the fibres suitable for linen. The hemp plant (cannabis sativia) would grow to a height of ten feet, but flax (linum usitatissimum) reached a height of just three to four feet. Both crops were grown in the open fields and most households were involved in either growing, spinning or weaving processes.

Women usually carried out the pulling of line (as flax was usually called) and hemp. Mr Peter Cranidge, a hemp and flax grower and dealer of nearby Crowle, kept a record of his work from 1773 to 1843 and it gives us an excellent insight to the industry in the area. The following are some typical entries:

Total amount of all flax grown on Cranidge Farm - 1787

| | | |
|---|---|---|
| Own. | 26 stone | £10. 8s. 0d |
| Mr Batty - Close under loam | 64½ stone | £25.16s. 0d |
| Swarthend in leases | 15½ stone | £6. 4s. 0d |
| Whiteline in leases | 29½ stone | £11. 1s. 3d |
| Seed in leases | 13 stone | £4. 17s. 6d |

August 29th, 1799. Paid for my line pulling to sundry pullers.    £1. 9s. 4d.
March 17th, 1799. Bought a quarter of line seed at £4.  14s. 6d (same day bought a hat at Epworth for 3s. 6d.)

At that time coat cloth was selling at 14s. 0d. per yard. Judging by the next two entries it would appear that there was not always a strict fairness in the paying of the wages.

| | | |
|---|---|---|
| August 17th, 1801. | Paid Polly Foster for three days spreading Lime - 3s. 0d. | |
| August 22nd, 1801. | Paid Anne Hampson for one day | - 2s. 0d. |
| | Paid Dolly Spenser for one day | - 2s. 0d. |
| May 6th, 1802. | Bought corduroy at Epworth market for 2s. 0d. a yard. | |
| October 6th, 1804 | Paid William Bellamy for 5½ days work thatching granary with flax (REF.4) | |

After harvesting about midsummer, the plants were either put to 'dew retting' for 20 to 30 days or were taken to pits for water retting which took 10 to 14 days (this process separated the fibres from the bark). It was an evil smelling business and the pits were usually sited well away from the village centre and in the case of Epworth, probably in the Burnham Skiers area. Traces of old retting pits can be seen on aerial photographs of East Lound where the land is still called 'The Rates', with other areas around Belton, Epworth and Haxey believed to have been retting sites. The best quality flax was sometimes retted twice.

The plants were dried for several weeks then scutched (beaten over a frame to remove waste from the fibres). Sometimes a device called a break was used for

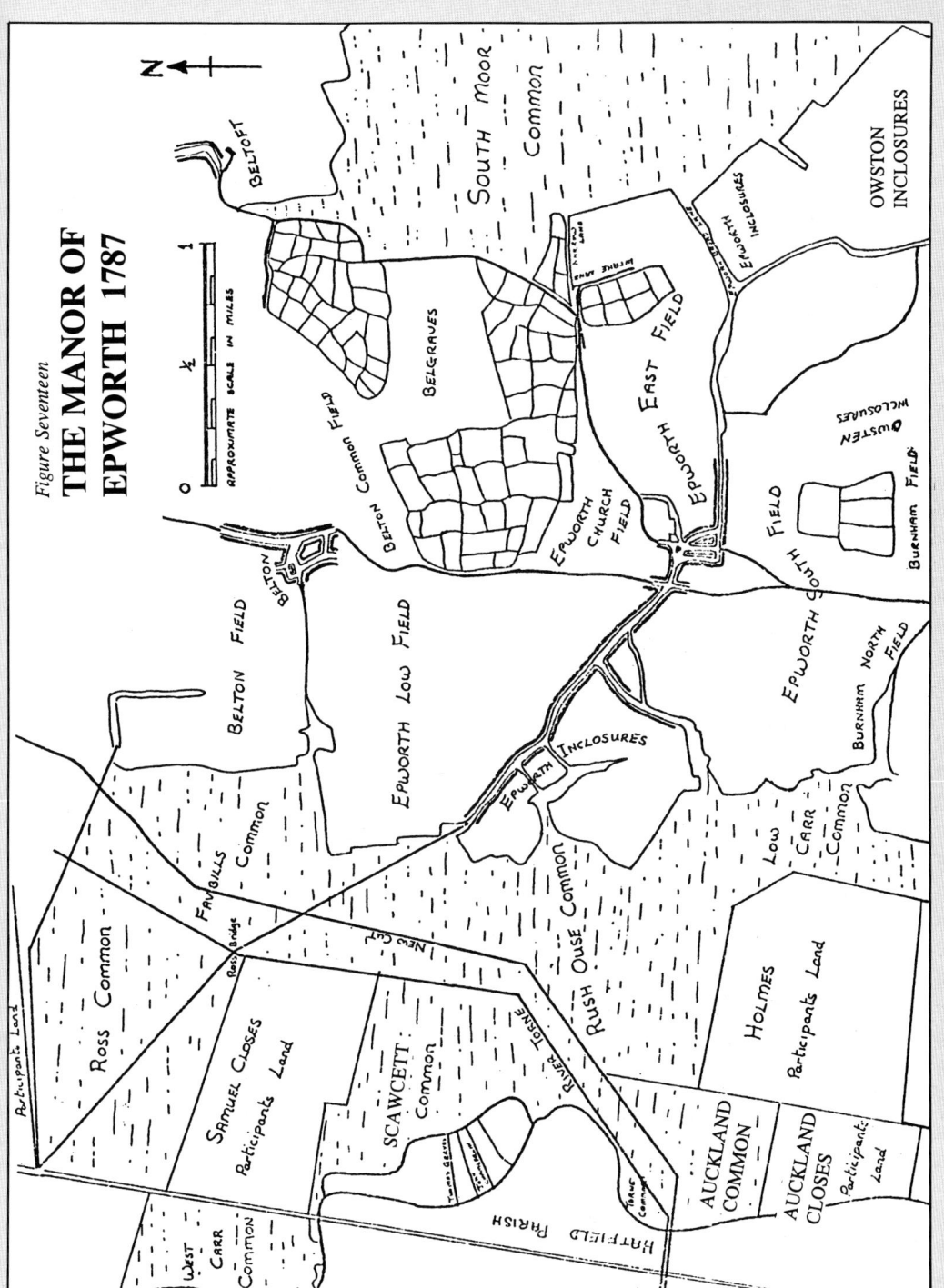

*Reproduced from P.A. Compton's unpublished Thesis, 'Epworth – Some Aspects of its Evolving Landscape'.*

this process - some of them being water driven. Next came the heckling when the fibres were pulled through an iron comb to straighten them.(REF.5)

Women and children spun the flax or hemp on a spinning wheel however in the medieval period it would have been spun by hand. Very early spinning wheels did not suit flax, but in the second half of the fifteeth century spinning wheels were made especially for the line. The treadle wheel came in the early 17th century and the two-handed treadle wheels were popular in the 1680's. Flax spinning was not fully mechanised until well into the nineteenth century.(REF.6)

Much of the yarn made in Epworth was of a coarse variety and was used in the making of wagon covers, grain bags, a variety of sacks, poor sheets and ropes. The industry declined late in the nineteenth century and moved to Crowle where there was a line mill still in use around the turn of this century.

Changes occurred rapidly in agriculture in the second half of the 18th century in efforts to eliminate what was, in many cases a wasteful, primitive and unprogressive system. During the reign of George III no less than 3,000 Enclosure Acts were passed involving over five and a half million acres of land. Enclosure now meant the merging of all land on the Manor including common, and the re-division amongst the commoners in proportion to their previous holdings on scattered strips. However just as they had resisted the drainage scheme so the Isleonians of Epworth and district were to oppose enclosure of their open fields.

As we have seen enclosure came to secure a more efficient and profitable use of land and so the Isle farmers were criticised for their lack of foresight and seeming inability to accept change. Stonehouse claimed that the Isle of Axholme had a greater number of land owners than any other part of Britain.(REF.7) Many smallholders had from 20 acres to just one rood and they were very poor and often worse-off than day labourers.

Isleonians have a reputation for resisting change born to some extent out of the historical and geographical development of Axholme, but enclosure was anything but new. It had gone on for centuries often with great abuse when areas had been de-populated by greedy land prospectors. It was carried out by the Earls of Lincoln in 1135 and 1225. In Tudor times sheep-rearing was so popular that acres of land were enclosed for it and even arable land was returned to pasture. This land-grabbing was prevalent on various estates throughout the 16th and 17th centuries and many small landowners lost out to the larger owners long before any official enclosure occurred.(REF.8)

In two periods, 1761 to 1780 and 1791 to 1810, about one third of the country was 'enclosed'. In Axholme these Enclosure Acts affected Wroot in 1775, Luddington and Garthorpe 1776, Amcotts 1779, parts of Owston, Haxey, Belton and Epworth in 1795 and Epworth again from 1799 to 1803. The town's Enclosure Awards were drawn up in 1803 and in them 100 acres of commonland for the turbaries was allotted to each of the four villages; Epworth, Belton,

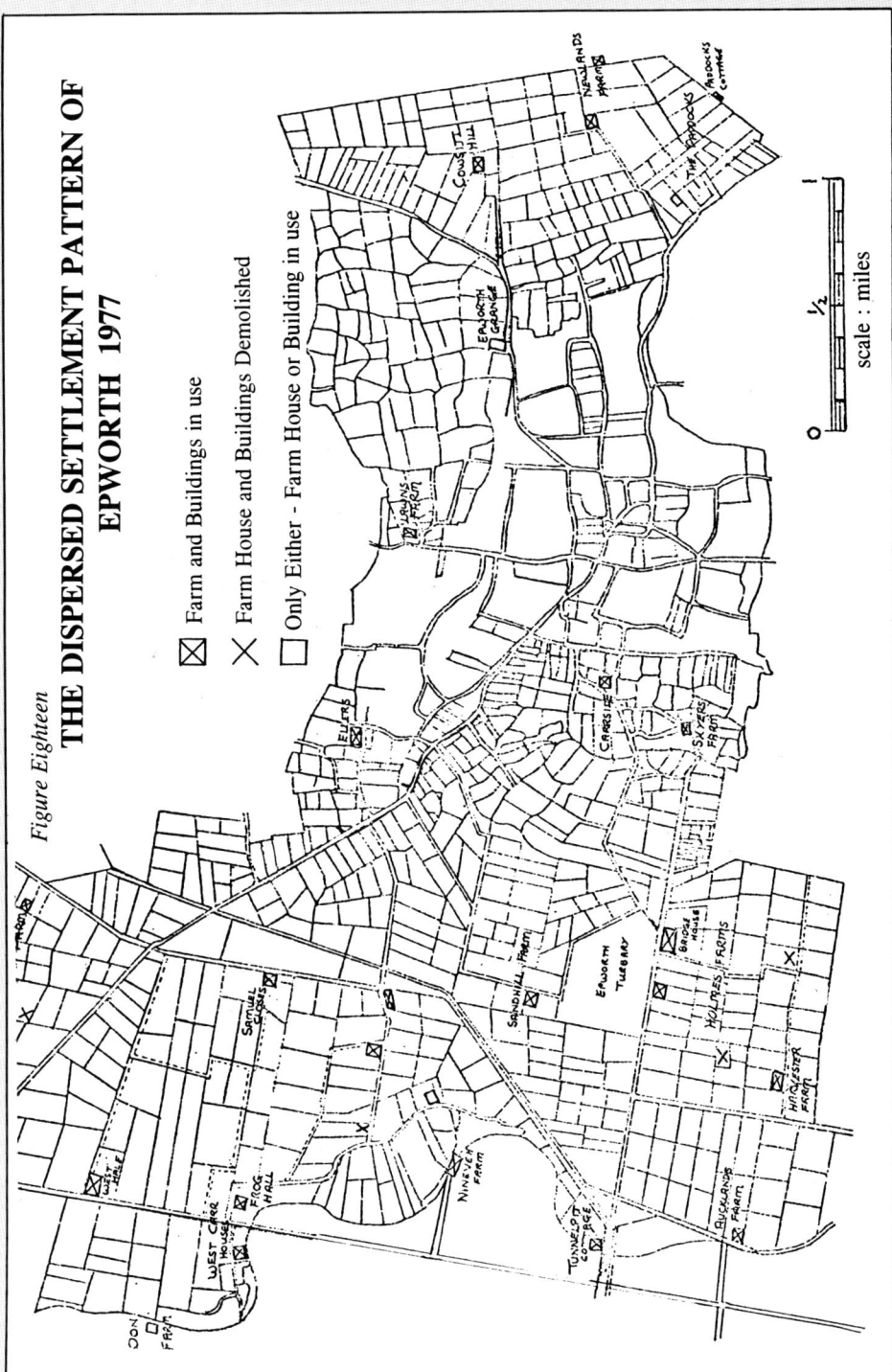

*Reproduced from P.A.Compton's unpublished Thesis, 'Epworth - 'Some Aspects of its Evolving Landscape'.*

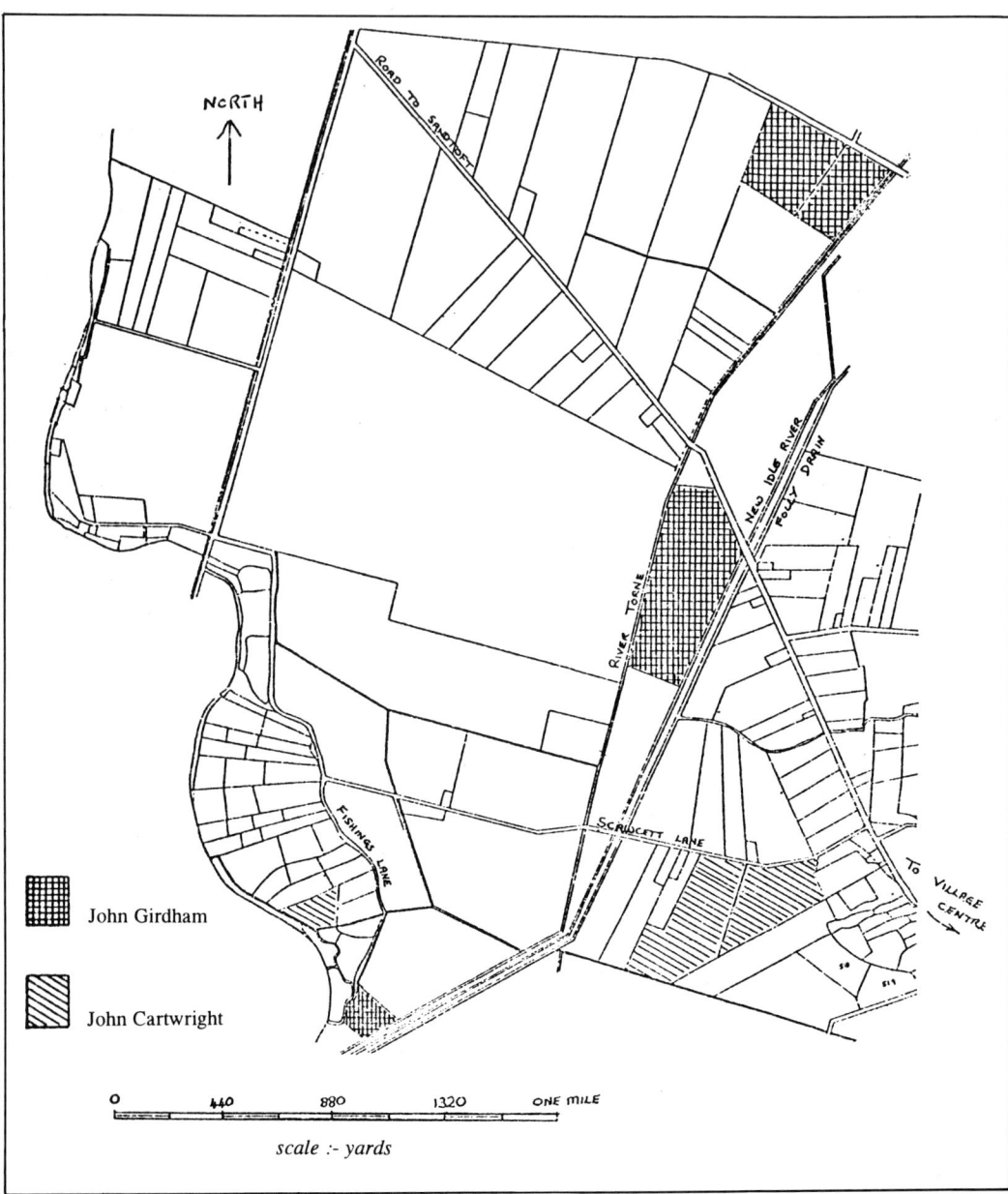

*Figure Nineteen*

**ENCLOSURES ALLOTTED TO**
John Girdham & John Cartwright

*Reproduced from P.A.Compton's unpublished Thesis,*
*'Epworth -'Some Aspects of its Evolving Landscape'.*

## AGRICULTURE AND ENCLOSURE

Haxey and Owston Ferry. Epworth Big Turbary then had 78½ acres and the Little Turbary 21½ acres.

Crowle had divided its two large fields into four as early as 1381 and those of Epworth of Ellers, Church, South and East may also date from about this time. Epworth's fields were divided into 1587 strips, but records suggest that this number may well fall short of the true figure. The Selions varied greatly in length and width due to the irregular shape of the furlongs and also because of the strips being combined, widened or lengthened. In order to aid drainage the strips were ploughed up and down the gradients; a feature that can readily be seen in looking at the slopes in Epworth's parish at the present time.(REF.9)

Copyholders with larger holdings often had land in all four fields whilst the smaller freeholders' allotments tended to have their land mostly in one of the larger fields, but with their strips scattered over a wide area. The coming of enclosure can often be seen in the long straight roads and tracks made through the affected area. In Epworth the enclosures mostly affected the low lying land to the east and west and the roads and access tracks are there seen to be very straight; the roads themselves having wide grass verges, as for example on the minor road from Epworth to Sandtoft. Occupation roads are frequently to be found joining public roads as at Nineveh Farm, Newlands Farm, Cowsitt Hill and other farms as seen in *Figure 18*.

The evolving field system on the commons as seen in *Figure 17* showing the 1787 Epworth Manor, suggests a developed lane pattern close to the village. Tracks then radiated out from the village centre, but all stopped at the edge of the common waste excepting that of the Sandtoft route which had probably been extended out to the Settlers' Headquarters in that village.

There seems to have been no real planning at all for many tracks and Broad Lane is a good example of a meandering lane used just for convenience. From very early times the farmers of Epworth possessed a right to fence and enclose an accumulated plot of five or six acres. This of course meant that rights of common were lost, but the land could still be grazed in common by cattle after the harvest. It seems that very few farmers had availed themselves of this facility in Epworth and furthermore when the Enclosure Acts were applied, the large open fields around the village escaped its working simply because the necessary majority of 75% of the freehold occupiers voting in favour, could not be obtained. Thus the fields around Belton, Epworth and Haxey have remained un-enclosed and survive even today as possibly one of the best examples of an open field system in this country. The system is however not taken so far as at Laxton in Nottinghamshire, for there amazingly enough the Court Leet still meets annually to administer the leases of its open fields.

Outside the area of Epworth's open fields, fences and hedges began to appear on the enclosed commons. Land was mostly offered to farmers in compact blocks, but not always so as can be seen in *Figure 19* in regard to the allotments to John

Girdham and John Cartwright. The smaller plots given were generally near the village - often bordering the roadside, whereas the larger ones were far out on common land. Two hundred years after Vermuyden, the Participant's land can still be seen in the Enclosure plans. *Figure 18* clearly illustrates many aspects of this period; the open fields are plain to see as are the smaller fields near the roadside and the larger ones inland.

It is of interest to compare the 1787 map of Epworth Manor in *Figure 17* with the settlement pattern of the 1977 field layout in *Figure 18*. It shows how the former commons were enclosed to become eventually excellent farm land. Two hundred years ago the farms were in the village itself and the built up area is indicated by the black lines along Epworth's streets. It was some years before farmers who had been awarded land on the commons, built homes in their own fields as shown in the 1977 map.

Strip farming continued then at Epworth through the 19th century, and gradually the plots increased in size and became fewer but even so holdings in Axholme were still considerably smaller than those in the Levels and on the Marshlands. All the villages of the Isle had many farmers and in Epworth around the 1850's, there were no less than 83 with 50 of these being land owners. In the 1930's Kelly's Lincolnshire Directory still lists 60 farmers in the Epworth parish and yet only Emerson Brown and Richard Selby farmed more than 150 acres.(REF.10) At this time statistics in Lindsey revealed that there were 1911 holdings of 1 to 5 acres; 3056 of 5 to 20 acres; 1979 of 20 to 50; 1370 of 50 to 100; 1013 of 150 to 300 and just 611 farms of over 300 acres.

Farming in a small way has been very much the order of the day around Epworth for centuries prolonged by the retention of the open field system. Warping many acres greatly improved soil conditions and potatoes were once grown on a grand scale in Axholme until the Boston district gained the monopoly in regard to this crop.

The conservative Isleonian farmers remained obdurate and slow to change and very few outsiders were able to enter the agricultural scene in Axholme. One big change in the late 19th century and the early 20th, was a rush into market gardening and consequently carrots, onions and turnips were grown in abundance with celery achieving something of a National reputation. Locally supplied gypsum was used as a soil conditioner and with other mixtures as a fertiliser.

The fragmentation of holdings in Axholme had nevertheless made for a lot of inefficient use of land. One farmer owned 40 acres in 100 different plots and many instances like this cannot have made for the most profitable use of the acreage. Smallholders struggled along on a pittance; even those with largish acreages sometimes suffering a lower standard of living than their employees.

Agriculture has remained a dominating concern in Epworth, but still remains a struggle for some businesses. Potatoes have again been a major crop and sugar beet too has been grown in quantity. Oilseed rape is a common sight and even flax is back in favour again. The red beetroot is a common crop in the lower levels of Epworth, Haxey, Owston Ferry and Wroot.

In general then, imaginative progress in agriculture was not forthcoming for 200 years after Vermuyden, but with the Enclosures, even though Epworth did retain its open fields, the situation could not long remain unaffected by the general improvement. Through all the ups and downs, successes and failures, gains and losses, the industry has weathered the storm. These days mechanisation has moved in and very large concerns now operate with a handful of employees making it hard to imagine the droves of farm labourers who once toiled in Epworth's fields.

REFERENCES
1. Cory, V. (1985) op. cit.
2. Tuffrey, P. *Streetwise. Old Doncaster Memories.* Doncaster Star, 1993.
3. *White's Lincolnshire Directory.* 1856.
4. *Notes on the Cranidge Papers.* Isle of Axholme Research Team. Humberside Archaeology Unit, 1988.
5. *Flax and Hemp Fact Sheet.* Humberside Archaeology Unit, 1988.
6. *Unpublished notes on Hemp and Flax.* Humberside Archaeology Unit, 1988.
7. Stonehouse, W.B. (1839) op. cit.
8. Brears, C. (1940) op. cit.
9. Crompton, P.A. *Thesis. Epworth. some Aspects of its Evolving Landscape.* Padgate College of Higher Education. 1977. Courtesy of the Mechanics' Institute at Epworth.
10. *Kelly's Lincolnshire Directory.* 1933.

## FLAX and HEMP PROCESSING

Scutching Flax or Hemp fibres.

Breaking Hemp.

Spinning Flax.

Heckling fibres.

*Illustrations by Permission of the Humberside Archaeology Unit.*

A view of Queen Street in the 'Good Old Days'. *Courtesy of Miss Marjorie Trimingham*

Early this century the High Street General Store on the left was owned by Mr W.A.Buttrick. It passed on to Tommy Goodman and then on to M.C.Trimingham, the brother of the supplier of this old postcard, Miss Marjorie Trimingham.

# CHAPTER EIGHT

## Local Affairs 1630 to 1830

Epworth's Manor Court continued to function until the present century, but Read says that even in 1858, most of the former business of this Court had devolved upon the Quarter Sessions.(REF.1) The Rolls of this Court are now kept in the Lincolnshire Archives, some of them, being so fragile, that they cannot be produced for the public. There is an interesting story in regard to the Manor Court's Records. During the Civil War, no doubt like many other things, the Court Rolls were lost, but Allan Johnson came across some of them in a shop in Newark where they were apparently being used as wrapping paper! So it was that documents dating back to Henry VIII were restored to Epworth.

The Lindsey Quarter Sessions were trying Epworth's law breakers in the 17th century and on the 24th June,1625, John Fair presided over the indictment of one Gilbert of Epworth who was charged with *'refusing to find one able-bodied man to keep watch from sunset to sunrise (as laid down by custom and Statute of the Parliament of Edward I)'* Edward Hewitson came before the Sessions for being a common gossip and for stirring up lawsuits and causing affrays and fights at Epworth on the 1st June,1633. (REF.2) A case of after hours drinking was brought against John Rose, an Epworth Ale House keeper, for allowing John Starkey and Alexander Starkey to drink on the Sabbath day (in the hymn of divine service) being the 15th May,1625. We find Simon Mawe, senior, a Yeoman, late of Epworth, charged with stealing an ewe worth 6s.0d. and a lamb worth 8d which was the property of Thomas Spilsworth. (REF.3)

The Vestry was the governing body of Epworth parish and they held their meetings at the west end of St Andrew's Church. They appointed Churchwardens, Petty Constables, Overseers of the Poor, Waywardens. Neatherds, Swineherds, Haywards, Pinders, Field Reeves and Dyke Reeves, although the last named were sometimes appointed by the Court of Sewers. The open Vestry meetings were attended by the ratepayers, but the Select Vestry would meet to deal with more confidential matters.

As early as 1563 a poor Law Act wanted collections for the poor and the appointing of two able-bodied persons in each Parish to collect them. In 1572 the office of Overseer of the Poor was created and by the end of the 16th century a Poor Rate was being levied and workhouses were built, whilst the Poor Law Act of 1601 established custom in respect of pauper relief which lasted until the Poor Law Amendment Act of 1834. The 1601 Act said that able-bodied people had to be found work whilst the impotent poor and malingerers would be put in the workhouse, and by 1776 there were some 2,000 workhouses in operation countrywide.

The Red Lion Inn is a very old resident of Epworth's Market Place having stood there since the mid 18th century. It still has its adjoining range of stables, granary and coach and carriage entrance. John Wesley is known to have lodged here.

'Glen House' in the High Street dates from 1779 and is a fine example of a period family house. Mr William Standring, a much appreciated resident of Epworth, lived here in the early years of this century. He was Epworth's Representative on the Board of Guardians for 27 years, becoming Chairman in 1905. He attended 489 meetings at Thorne, frequently walking the 20 miles round trip, until he bought a bicycle.

The Justices of the Peace played a leading role in local government and although some were idle and inefficient, most of them did the job fairly and well, and frequently showed commendable feeling for the lot of the poor and needy. The Rev Caley Illingworth, who was later to become Rector of Epworth, was indefatigable in his work. Like many other magistrates, he often did his utmost to mitigate the severity of the law. When Samuel Bamford and other radicals were confined in Lincoln Castle, Illingworth and his associates made every effort to make the prisoners (whose opinions they detested) as comfortable as possible and had them treated with every indulgence. (REF.4)

The duties of the JP were extremely wide ranging for they concerned themselves with all kinds of Rates; the licensing of churches and chapels; prices, weights and measures, fraud, theft, trespass, swearing, Sabbath breaking, deportation, settlements, road building and repair and shipwrecks. Examples of their work in certain parts of Lincolnshire are given below and they illustrate matters likely to have occurred in or near Epworth as well.

| | |
|---|---|
| 1708. | Ordered William Norris of Bardney putt down from selling ale it being proved his being very drunk and allowing other disorders in his house. |
| 1732. | The Keeper of the Louth House of Correction to be fined £5 for suffering Jonathan Parrott to escape. |
| 1737. | Presentments against Thomas Brown of South Willingham for rescue of 200 sheep, John Dolland of Sturton in the Street for not keeping watch and ward, John Watts of Scunthorpe for building a house upon the common, and the Constable of Carlton Parva for the pound (pinfold) being out of repair (also 132 persons for drawing ale without a licence) |
| 1743. | Edmund Nun, late of Gainsborough, Labourer, fined £10 for defrauding (several men at Crowle and Luddington) of several sums of money at Crowle Fair at Cups and Balls, otherwise Bilbow Catch. |
| 1776. | Ordered that all churchwardens and Overseers of the Poor be very vigilant and strict in prosecuting (Sabbath breakers). Warrants sent to Chief Constables and Petty Constables to search for and apprehend immediately all rogues etc. |
| 1780. | John Coggan of Belton, Coroner, fined 40s for holding an inquisition at Belton on the body of a man who died at Gainsborough. (REF.5) |

It was the local Petty Constable who presented law-breakers at the Quarter Sessions and amongst his other duties he had to execute warrants, organise the watch, arrange for the custody and care of Parish property; administer punishment at the stocks and the pillory and keep pinfolds, bridges, fences and gates in good order. One job that went from the Church-warden to the Constable was the destruction of vermin. People were given cash rewards for hedgehogs, foxes, rat's tails and sparrows, and the last named were slaughtered in tremendous numbers.

The Constable had to see that drainage work was in order and he had also to raise Militia as required. One of his most difficult jobs was dealing with wandering tramps and vagrants. Judging by some entries in Court Records, the

The Market Place in the early 1900's with the old 17th century King's Head Hotel at the top of the street - a place where Samuel Wesley quenched his thirst. Bottom left is Emerson's Furniture shop.
*Courtesy of Edwin Harrison*

The former Old Free School in High Street, dating from 1711 which used to stand in the vicinity of the present day School Close. *Reproduced from 'Epworth What to See and How To Get There' A Lancashire & Yorkshire Railway Booklet, 1905.* *Courtesy of Miss Marjorie Trimingham.*

Constables, in many cases, must have found writing something of a burden. We see reports like *'for Righten ought dublecats- 2s.0d'*; it translates *'for writing out duplicates'*, but I will let you work out this one *'Pade for lad goin to Housaker recttion- 1s.0d.*(REF.6)

The population of Epworth in 1801 was 1434 and if we assume a growth rate similar to that of the Victorian period, then its population during the time of the Wesleys was probably somewhere between 1100 to 1200. Again if we assume that families may have had on average four or five members, we can see that Epworth may have had somewhere between 300 to 350 houses, most of them in an area stretching a mile or so between Rectory Street and roughly the end of the Station Road area, therefore the Town officials we are looking at would have been dealing with far fewer householders than we know today.

In the early 16th century many of these homes would have been wooden framed with thatched roofs, but increasingly bricks would certainly have been in use at this time. Techniques of brick and tile making were copied from the Dutch and became important industries in districts bordering the Humber and also in parts of Axholme. Pantiles were made at nearby Hatfield in 1704 and some of these could well have been used on houses in Epworth. The new materials brought more variety in the shape and size of houses; glass appeared in windows and doors became a central feature, sometimes having canopies and pillars. Inside, stone floors were laid and wall paper was in use by the mid 18th century. The ladders and stone steps were replaced with wooden staircases, which, in the better homes, were often of the dog leg or well styles.

Of course such progress brought the inevitable taxation and the Hearth Tax, imposed by the Cavalier Parliament acting under Charles II in 1662, meant that anyone who owned property rated at 20s a year or more and who was not exempt through poverty or in receipt of alms or relief, was liable to pay an annual tax of 2s for every fireplace or stove. It was a most unpopular imposition and in fact, only survived for 27 years. The window tax was levied from 1697 until 1851 and was charged on houses with more than six windows. It is possible, even here in Epworth, to see where old houses have had window spaces blocked up to avoid some of this tax. The Brick Tax, introduced by George III's Prime Minister, William Pitt, in 1784 lasted until 1850. All this, on top of Church Rates, General Rates, Poor Rates, Tithes and other taxes must have been pretty hard on the pocket. The average life span was much shorter than that we see today and people did well to get into their sixties. Children were frequently lost in childbirth, or if they survived that, they often died after a few years.

Susannah Wesley's losing nine of her children was not at all remarkable and it is something of a miracle that ten of her nineteen offspring survived to reasonable ages. In one of her letters to her son John, written from Wroot in September, 1724, the famous mother tells him that she was the only member of her family who had escaped the smallpox. Her experience is borne out by the Epworth

Some idea of the tranquillity of life at the turn of the century can be gathered from this homely scene on the Belton Road looking towards Epworth, with Brook's Mill on the right in full sail.

*Reproduced from 'Epworth and its Surroundings, 1903.*

The same scene nearly a century later and even today the only change here is a better road with modern houses replacing the old dwellings. The mill itself has been made into an attractive residence.

Parish Registers which for 1724 record twelve deaths in July alone, as against the usual average of just two in that month over many years. It was often a rare thing to see a face not marked by this disease and Queen Mary died of it in 1694.

Before and after the period we are considering the Market Place was the focal point of the town. No doubt there were more ale houses in it or adjacent to it in the Georgian era and the former inn, the King's Head, is believed to date from 1679. We know that John Wesley stayed at the Red Lion and his father would often slack his thirst in the King's Head after he had given his sermon. References to drinking offences are extremely common in the Quarter Sessions Records, amply bearing out the fact that facilities for that pastime were many. Of course, we must remember that small ale was the normal household beverage in those days. The Market Place must have witnessed many a scene of rough and tumble around its pillory and stocks as the unfortunate victims received the mob's catcalls and abuse. John Wesley is reputed to have turned back on seeing Cock Fighting in the Market Place and found an alternative route to the Church.

Roadways of any quality were few and far between in Wesley's day. Once the traveller reached the commons beyond the open fields, he could often go no further without great difficulty. In order to get from Epworth to Wroot there were times when the Wesleys had to take a boat at Scawcett Bridge to reach that village. The road network had changed little from that seen on the Hatfield Chace map (included earlier) and Stonehouse tells us that the local tracks of the 18th century were in a very bad state and that in winter they were impassable, even on horseback. Causeways had been laid of Yorkshire flags, (wide enough for a horse to walk on) first in the villages themselves and then, round about 1810, further afield connecting one village to another. By 1840 better roads, sixteen to eighteen feet wide were built, but the causeways remained making useful pathways and on these it was possible to walk the entire length of Axholme. The improved roads meant that agricultural loads could be moved in greater bulk with fewer horses at a quarter of the cost.

Epworth's Highways Account from the early years of the 19th century, lists twenty people on the Turbary using eighteen plots. It was one of the areas tended by John Pilsworth, who in 1805, was the Surveyor of the Private Roads and Public Drains. In that year the expense incurred in maintaining them was £43.19s. 0d; in 1806 it was £14. 10s. 0d and in 1807 it amounted to £18 2s. 0d. During 1824 Pilsworth was succeeded by John Brunyee and the records show that payments to numerous individuals were made for the upkeep of drains, bridges and roads. In 1835 Brunyee's son is appointed, and ten years later the position is in the hands of Samuel Clark, whose expenses for that year were £8. 14s. 0d.

From this Committee we learn that they held their various meetings in the White Bear, Red Lion, Queen's Head and the Half Moon. The *'Epworth Town Trail'* tells us that Epworth once had some thirteen retail outlets for alcoholic drink and the premises of the former Royal Oak and the Gate Inn are now private houses. For decade after decade the Surveyor's salary stood at two guineas, but reached three guineas in 1876.(REF.7)

A 1901 account of charities in Epworth records Richard Brewer's gift dated 11th November,1687, in which he leaves his entire estate, Halifax Farm, to dispose of the rents thereof yearly *'towards clothing so many ancient poor people of Epworth'*. A Parish Book entry gives the acreage of Brewer's farm as 11 acres and 13 perches, lying in 13 small plots in Epworth Field. In 1702 Robert Whiteley gave a plot of 1 rood, 20 perches, in the same field to be used for the same purpose.

The Manor Court in December,1713, records that Richard Coggan had given a parcel of land in the East Field described as four selions containing one acre *'to the use of the poor of Epworth parish.'*

Ann Maw, by a will dated 26th March,1810 left £40 to be laid out by her executors in land from which the rent could be given to poor families and widows in Epworth.

Several other charities existed under the names of Robert Whiteley (senior), Edmund Whitelam, Henry Whiteley, Henry Bird and William Thorpe, for which there had never been any official surrender or admission. Nevertheless, the Churchwardens administered these trusts from which a total of £37. 3s. 0d. a year was raised for charity.

In all, from Poor Lands' rent and various bequests the Churchwardens and Overseers of Epworth's poor received £43. 13s. 4d. annually and it was disposed of as follows every year.

| | | |
|---|---|---|
| Ashmell's will | - to orphan children. | £1. 0s. 0d. |
| Maw's bequest | - to widows | £2. 0s. 0d. |
| Coggan's dole and others unknown | - to widows. | £2. 0s. 0d. |
| In articles of clothing. | | £37. 13s. 4d. |

The Charity record tells how clothing distribution was arranged. *'A certain number of poor persons are selected, to each of whom a ticket for 5s is given, as far as the funds will allow, which ticket is exchangeable at certain specified shops in Epworth, for such articles as the party pleases, either linen, woollen or cloth; and the tickets are allotted to all the dealers in the town, in proportion to the value on which they are rated, for their stock-in-trade, it being the custom at Epworth to pay poor rates for the amount of such stock.'*

The Record then mentions gifts of money from Mr J.C. Hill, Mr W.B. Rhodes and Miss Wilkinson which had been left since their list of charities had been compiled.(REF.8)

In regard to the educational scene in those days, undoubtedly there would have been many people who were illiterate or semi-illiterate and many of the records of those times often show spelling of an appalling standard.

It is possible that some Epworth lads may have received some education in the Chantry Chapels of the 14th century or from the monks at the nearby Carthusian monastery at Low Melwood. Some of the better off may have sent their sons to the grammar schools which were in existence at Louth, Lincoln, and Grimsby as early as the 14th century.

Petty Schools for infants and Dame Schools for young children were common all over the country in the 16th century and even earlier. Epworth, like many other towns, seems to have had a good selection of private academies and even boarding schools. Samuel Wesley (junior), attended John Holland's Academy in Epworth, a master, who, like Samuel Wesley (senior), was once a prisoner in Lincoln Castle Gaol. Early in the 19th century Owston Ferry had a Dame School at which fourteen girls were taught to read and sew. The Mistress was paid £11 12s. 0d. per annum.

Village schools often have very long histories and were frequently endowed by private persons. Reading and writing was the staple diet on the curriculum, but Accounts too were taught to help in Apprenticeships. The standard of teaching was sometimes not the most to be desired and we read of John Wilkinson at Belton in 1788, who had been a farm labourer before taking up teaching. He was sacked after just three months and removed from the Parish. In the same year, on the other hand, Thomas Gervase, the Epworth Schoolmaster was appointed Chief Constable of the Manley Wapentake. (REF.9)

A memorandum from Epworth's Manorial Count Rolls in 1838 tells how the Free School (which used to stand in the High Street) came into being in 1711. It records how Henry Clifford, the Rector of Wroot surrendered his property on the south side of Queen Street to the use of George Whichcot, Samuel Wesley, Rector of Epworth, Robert Coggan, John Marr (junior), Joshua Whiteby, John Urry (junior) and Peter Barnard, the trustees who had been elected by those who had subscribed to the purchasing of a schoolhouse.

Gifts that helped maintain the school came from Richard Coggan's will of 1713 in which he left an estate with a rent charge of 40s for the use and maintenance of the schoolmaster; from Charles Kelsey's gift of a two rod plot in Epworth Field in 1728 and from an acre of land donated by Ann Crosland. As a result of the Enclosures at Epworth, the Commissioners awarded to the Trustees of the School an allotment containing three acres, three rods and two perches in the right of the house and premises occupied by the schoolmaster. All these contingencies raised £16 0s. 0d per year in land and property rents and ensured that the school fulfilled the purposes for which it had been provided.(REF.10)

Possibly much credit for the coming of this early educational venture must go to the Rev Samuel Wesley, for the Epworth Rector made every effort to get a school established; seeking to obtain assistance from the Society for the Promotion of Christian Knowledge and fully acquainting them with the desperate need of his parishioners. He also contacted many influential people and yet, for all this, most of the funds for the school came from the benevolence of his own church members.

At the beginning of the 19th century the Master was William Gervas who it appears had some sort of unseemly dispute with the Trustees which entailed Court proceedings. In 1803 he was succeeded by Mr Thomas Addey who was Master for 26 years. After him came Mr Thomas Bailey Pearson who took up his appointment in 1829. In his time the school rules were;

1) That the number of free scholars be fixed at 20 and that the gratuitous education of that number be restricted to reading.

2) That the children on the foundation shall be taught writing, if required, at the rate of 3s per quarter, to be paid by their parents.

3) That no child be admitted to the school except at a quarterly meeting of the Trustees and that application for such admission be made to the Master at least seven days before such meeting, to be by him reported to the Trustees.

4) That the children on the foundation be required to attend Divine Service in the Church at Epworth on Sunday mornings, under the superintendence of the Master.

5) No child to remain more than three years on the foundation.

There was a strict adherence to the number of 20 pupils, but the Master could supplement his income, and often did, by private tuition. In 1901 it was said that most of the men of Epworth past middle life, had received some education at this school and that there were men all over the world who kept a warm corner in their hearts for that quaint old building and its memories. (REF.11)

Epworth's Poor House was next to Mr. Barnard's house in Queen Street in the early years of the 18th century and some sort of Pauper Institution could well have dated from an even earlier time. Overseers of the Poor had been appointed in 1597 and at least two people were appointed yearly by each Vestry with the approval of the Justices of the Peace. After 1834, Overseers became just assessors and collectors of the Poor Rate and their former other duties were given to the Guardians of the Poor. At the beginning of the 17th century they collaborated with the Churchwardens in providing relief for the poor and attempts to find such relief figure prominently in records of this time. The origin of many Turbaries lies in these areas, being given for the use of the poor and those at Epworth, Owston and Belton are such examples.

The workhouses were often very grim places as many instances in literature depict and in all likelihood those of Axholme were no exception. Epworth has its sinister tale of Poll Pilsworth who was employed as a keeper at the Poorhouse. She is reputed to have poisoned a number of inmates by contaminating some flour from which bread was made, the action resulting in a number of deaths. When Poll's evil action came to light she poisoned herself and it was said that she was buried near the junction of Burnham Road and Blow Row, and that two stakes were driven through her body - a custom used for murderers. (REF.12)

Another Epworth elaboration of this grim tale claims that footsteps can be heard pounding down Gypsy Lane, the track by the side of Epworth's Parish Cemetery, and another spot thought to be the place of Poll's burial. Indeed in the *'Epworth*

*Town Trail'* booklet, the Epworth Society say that at least one local resident has heard running footsteps in the night for which there was no logical explanation.

The coming of the 1834 Poor Law Amendment Act saw Parishes amalgamated into 'unions' to provide for the poor. A common workhouse was provided and Althorpe, Amcotts, Keadby, Belton, Crowle, Epworth, Wroot and Eastoft, all sent their paupers, vagrants and sometimes petty offenders to Thorne Workhouse, whilst Luddington and Garthorpe used the Goole Institution and poor folk from Haxey, Owston Ferry and West Butterwick were sent to the Gainsborough Workhouse. (REF.13)

REFERENCES
1. Read, W.         (1858) op.cit.
2. *Notes on Lindsey Quarter Sessions.* Lincolnshire Archives.
3. Ibid.
4. Brears, C.       (1940) op.cit.
5. Ibid.
6. Ibid.
7. *Highway Accounts. 1816-1878.* Lincolnshire Archives.
8. Beal,Thomas.    *Charities of the Isle of Axholme.* 1901.
9. Brears, C       (1940) op.cit.
10. Beal, T.       (1901) op.cit.
11. Ibid.
12. Messiter,A.F.  (1912) op.cit.
13. *White's Lincolnshire Directory.* 1842.

The window tax levied on houses with more than six windows from the 17th to the 19th centuries was not popular and many people blocked in windows to avoid paying it. Examples of this avoidance can be seen in various parts of Epworth and this picture shows where windows have been blocked on a property forming part of the present *'Axholme Landscapes'* business in West End Road. It is believed that this house was once an old coaching inn.

Epworth's medieval Market Cross. John Wesley preached from it many times, at a time when it was positioned a little distance to the left of this view. Then it was surmounted by a slender stone pillar topped with a cross.

'The Grange' on Epworth's High Street. More elderly residents will remember this house serving as the Grange Collegiate School - one of several private and quite select educational establishments in the town.

# CHAPTER NINE

## The Victorian Scene

To write about changes and developments in Epworth through the 19th century would require a substantial book in itself and in the context of this work an attempt is made to chart some of the salient points of progress through this varied and eventful period. It was still the time of master and man; the days of the Lord of the Manor and a time when the Manor Courts were still held twice a year in the Market Place Court House.

But the ordinary man was striving to better his situation; to improve his education and this can be seen in the use of the facilities of the Mechanics' Institute and in evening classes. Mechanics' Institutes were pioneered by George Birkbeck, when he (along with others) founded the London Mechanics' Institute in 1823.

The printer and writer of the well known 1858 *'History of Axholme'*, William Read, was a member of the London Mechanics' Institute, and when he returned to Epworth he established in 1837 such an Institute in the town, which in its early period, operated in a room at the back of Read's shop in Albion House. After 1839 the Institute saw itself housed in many different places and at one time it was even operating in the archway leading into Albion House. At a later time it made use of the Temperance Hall premises. As time went by the Institute grew in popularity and had an excellent supply of books, newspapers and journals. Funds for its maintenance were raised by a regular round of concerts, plays, soirees and charades.

The Mechanics' Institute today is accommodated on the first floor of the Manor Court House in the Market Place. The present writer, having spent many hours of research there, can vouch for its being a valuable asset for the town and it has a fine collection of older fiction as well as modern and also a most interesting range of factual material. Any student of local history will find the Institutes' archive material invaluable. (REF.1)

Outside the Courthouse stands the Market Cross - a listed monument from which, according to the plaque on it, John Wesley preached. He did - but not quite from that position. At one time roads passed all round the cross and in 1806, it was re-positioned a short distance further north. Whether the original stones were replaced I cannot say, but at any rate the cross was refurbished at the time of this movement. It was Alexander Johnson, the Lord of the Manor who carried out this work. In those days the cross had a stone pillar surmounting it which survived until the 1890's, when some years later it was embellished with a decorative three-pillar ornamental ironwork around and above the cross. Each of the pillars bore the inscription *'Erected by public subscription to commemorate the Coronation of Edward VII'* and for those of you who know your history, that

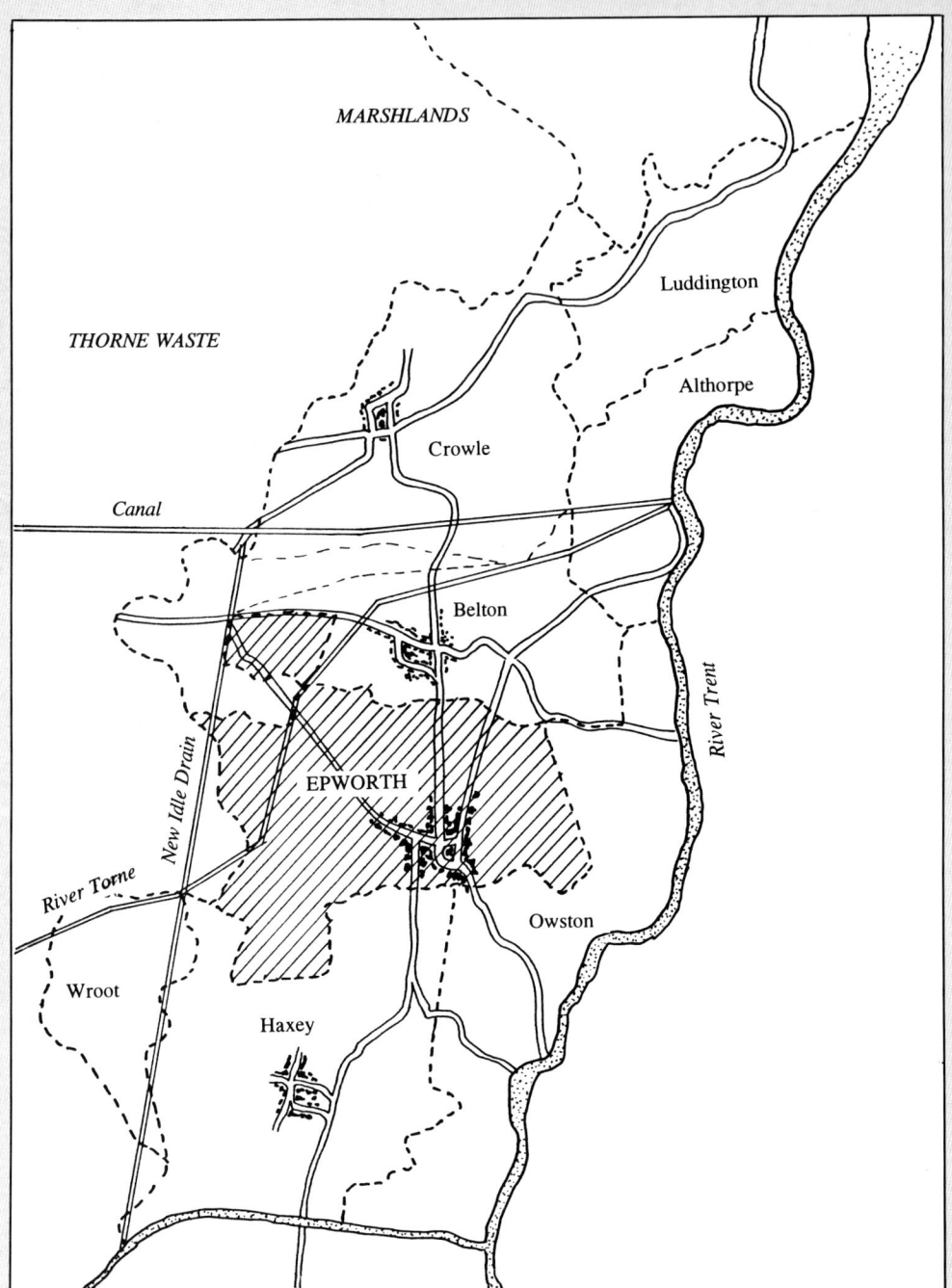

*Figure Twenty*
A simplified section of a map found in Read's History of the Isle of Axholme showing the extent of the Epworth Parish in 1857 in relation to the other parishes in Axholme and also showing just a little of the then developing road networks.

The Old Board School in Battle Green with its distinct polychromatic brickwork, closed in 1982 after serving the community for 106 years. The short square tower was earlier surmounted by a pointed bell spire. It can plainly be seen how the building is used today!

The Magistrates' Court in Hollingsworth Lane has served Epworth since 1848. The Senior Police Officer's house was once attached to it, but a 1983 extension to the court saw that house disappear. At the same time two new police houses were erected alongside.

gives you the date. This ironwork disappeared around the time of the Second World War and the cross has twice received maintenance attention this century.(REF.2)

What had previously been a very busy market earlier in the 19th century declined in the late Victorian era and by the 1870's was a business that mainly saw the sale of butter, eggs and poultry. People were wanting a market room instead and although Mr Harrap was willing to let a room for such a purpose next to Lindley's shop, nothing came of it and gradually the long history of Epworth's market came to an end.

Epworth's population began to grow in the 19th century and by 1841 it had reached a total of 1843. It appears from Vestry minutes that there was still a good deal of poverty in the town and there were many applications for footwear and clothing. Judging by the number of people whose requests were turned down there may have been some abuse of the system. For example we read:

29th March 1836 - S.Slater applied for some clothing for her son Giles.

*Refused.*

23rd August, 1836- 'Susannah Fields applied for relief.

*Refused.'*

Movements to and from the workhouse are frequently recorded. In 1827 we find the Vestry reducing the rent of Simon Kilham because his factory (probably a textile one) had closed down some years earlier. From the following entry it can perhaps be assumed that medical services were not exactly generous. It is contained in the Vestry Minutes of the 16th April,1827 and reads: *'Ordered that the medical man in the parish be requested to send to the next Vestry Meeting sealed orders containing the lowest sum of which he will engage to do all the parish business in that line for one year'*. On the 24th December,1835, Henry Cooper was appointed as Parish mole catcher for ten years; to get eleven guineas for the first year, but only ten guineas a year for the next nine years.(REF.3)

All the fun and merriment of the fairs were part of the Victorian scene in Epworth market place. Belton too, had its Flax Fair on the 25th September and there was an abundance of goods at Haxey Feast on the 5th July, and Crowle held annual fairs in May, September and November as well as a biennial cattle fair in June. White's Directory records that Epworth held two fairs annually on the Thursday after Michaelmas Day and the Thursday after May Day, for the sale of cattle. Fairs of the 1890's had all kinds of stalls selling a variety of goods; there were swings, roundabouts, shooting galleries and troops of ponies. Something of the life and vigour of the fair can be seen in the capacity and digestion of the men of Axholme in this example of one of their early Victorian customs.

*A Challenge*
*to all the*
*Beef eaters in England.*
*Notice is hereby given, that*
*Ten men of Epworth will undertake to*

*Eat Beef*
*with*
*Any ten men in England*
*for*
*50 Pounds a Side*
*(Play or Pay)*
*on Thursday next 25th Day of September at Belton Fair.* (REF.4)

The market place was also the centre for the November hirings when men and boys would wait around to be hired for farm service. A boy's wages were 9 to 12 guineas a year and a man's from 19 to 26 guineas. Often, when it was a poor harvest such as in 1879, little hiring was carried out. Ten years later in 1889 there was a very poor attendance (particularly in the case of females) because of the coldness of the weather, but again, to some extent the hirings may have been in some decline even as early as that time.

The 1870's saw £55 set aside for the flagging of the town and there was a strong interest in improving the roads and causeways. The market place had been paved by York paviors in 1745 and also boulder stone from the old church at Wroot was used as paving in the 1790's. Roads gradually improved through the Victorian years and Epworth introduced a road sweeping machine which was worked with one or two horses. It had a large, circular revolving brush and was first used on the 12th March, 1873. In 1881, the Guardians of Thorne Workhouse were asking for the roads in Epworth's approaches to be repaired, thus giving able-bodied men work in winter instead of suffering hunger or even worse still-applying for parish relief. Between 1850 and 1900 (and earlier), good macadam roads had been built and round about the turn of the century Epworth was sharing the use of a steam roller with its neighbouring villages.

Well before the coming of the weekly *'Epworth Bells'* newspaper the town had the *'Epworth Herald'*. It was yet another creation of William Read who has been called 'the most diverse businessman and entrepreneur that Epworth has ever known'. His premises in Albion Hill stretched for some distance along that road and he sold everything from a pill to genuine blood manure plus being the printer of the *'Epworth Herald'* in the mid 19th century.

To return to the educational scene, the Victorian times witnessed the work of several academies, including a Ladies' Boarding and Day School. In the 1820's and later Miss M.J. Isle was offering instruction for young ladies in all branches of a social education in Mrs Capes' Schoolroom. The Grange Collegiate School was well known in those days and the house of that name 'The Grange' can still be seen in High Street today.

Many an Epworth resident may well have received some basic education from the very large Sunday Schools that were a feature of the 18th and 19th centuries. The 1851 Religious Census reveals that no less than 257 children attended the

The Temperance Hall, built in 1868, was owned by the United Kingdom Temperance Alliance not so many years ago. It is now privately owned and serves as offices for the editorial and advertising staff of the *Epworth Bells* as well as for other concerns. The very first moving pictures at Epworth were shown here.

Epworth's Parish Cemetery is tastefully positioned out along Burnham Road and has this eminently fitting entrance dating from 1881.

Sabbath Schools of the various sects and it is a well known fact that the Primitive Methodists in many areas did help their scholars with reading and writing.

Real educational strides were made in the 1840's when the Rev. Charles Dundas (a long serving, distinguished Epworth Rector and Chairman of the Board of Magistrates at Epworth for many years) was instrumental in bringing about the establishment of the National (Church) School in1845. It can still be seen just off to the right on entry into Church Walk and it serves today as a venue for various functions in the town. The plans for the school in 1844 went as far as to depict the type of benches to be fitted in the schoolroom, which were backless and arranged in rigid rows facing the teacher. By 1863, this school had 171 pupils and (wait for it), they were taught by one certified teacher and one pupil teacher. (REF.5)

The Old Free School was not to survive this competition, especially when the 1870 Education Act came along and all over the country, towns and villages were required to organise School Boards for the running of the new Board Schools that developed in that decade. Epworth's Board School with its polychromatic Brickwork (now an Inn in Battle Green) was opened on the 9th November,1876 and its charges were: 2d per week for children under 6; above 6 and under 8 - 3d per week; above 8 and under 10 - 4d per week and above 10 years old - 6d per week. Subjects taught were reading, writing, arithmetic, grammar, geography and the girls were also taught sewing.

There was a good deal of non-attendance, for children were often kept at home to do various jobs and the 1875 Education Act stated that children between 8 and 12 years of age were not to be employed in agricultural labour.

The Free School used to be known as Mr Pearson's school and he taught there for forty-five years. In its 169 years existence, it had served Epworth well, but now with two other schools in the town as well as private ones, it was not to survive. In July 1880, Mr Kirk, then Master of the Free School was appointed to the Board School and his pupils went with him. By 1905 his old school was reported to be in poor state of repair and falling down.

Canon Matthews, the Inspector for Religious Instruction visited the National School in May 1886 and was well pleased with the general progress of the pupils. In 1892 the Board School had 50 boys whilst the girls and infants totalled 80, and the National School had by then 115 scholars. Parents were sometimes summoned for not sending their offspring to school. A Belton pupil who had been constantly absent, was ultimately committed to the Industrial School at Leicester for cruelty to a fowl, where he was sentenced to stay for 6 years and thirteen days! (REF.6)

In 1901, William Dawson, a Cambridge graduate, was appointed Head of the National School and he was paid £115 per year. It seems that under a Miss Milner the school had not been too successful. By 1904, both of Epworth's schools were funded by the District Council, a business which caused some

# EPWORTH

*Figure 21*

The First Edition of the 25" Ordnance Survey Map dated 1886 of Epworth Town Centre
*Courtesy Ordnance Survey*

Church Walk - Some time between the Great War and World War Two.

controversy in the Church School, mainly over the question of Religious Instruction.

A fire engine was provided in 1868, this being manually operated and horse drawn, and stored in the outbuilding that still stands at the rear of the Manor Court House. (REF.7) It may not have been too successful for a book about that very eccentric character of Hatfield, Jack Hawley, tells how the horse-drawn fire-engine from Doncaster made a journey to Epworth in the record time of one hour and five minutes on its way to deal with a fire at Mr. Sisson's barn.

The poor Rate was levied right through the 19th century and in 1845 at a rate of 10d in the pound a total of £288. 6s. 0¼d was requested. The Overseers were Richard Hill and Thomas Clough. People paid up pretty well for the Overseers actually received £278. 16s. 6½d. The Rate Book Record was signed by the Churchwardens, Henry Maw and John Bower and the whole account was endorsed by two Justices of the Peace; the Rev W. B. Stonehouse and Richard Sheffield. By 1890 the Rate stood at 16d and a total of £471. 18s. 6d was collected. A bigger rise might have been expected, but in fact Epworth's population fell from 2295 in 1871 to only 1856 in 1901. No doubt this was due to people obtaining work further afield; fewer temporary settlers and also the fact that domestic servants were in decline.

The first Edition of the 25" Ordnance survey map of Epworth Town Centre for 1886 (late Victorian) shows the age old street layout converging on the Market Place. Some streets we know now are not named here, such as Greengate, Mowbray Street, Blow Row and Battle Green, whilst Rectory Street was called Pinfold Street and Back Street, the latter also forming the present Mowbray Street. The town centre was heavily ribbon developed even then and today most of the gaps have been filled in with further housing. It can be seen that at this time the present Greengate, Blow Row, Burnham Road and Fieldside had very few houses while Tottermire Lane had the Gas Works and some other buildings at its western end.

It can readily be seen that many of the properties were the small cottage type, often built for people that worked at the textile or leather factories. In the main such houses have now suffered demolition as in the cases of those that once stood in Batley's Yard, Bramhill's Yard, and near the High Street/Belton Road Crossroads. This map indicates a good deal of backfilling and no doubt such buildings would have housed many of the trades prevalent in Epworth then, which are listed in *Table 3*. Some of these would have been used in the processing of hemp and flax and at a later time for the tanning and processing of leather.

Footpaths are shown along all the main thoroughfares and then there are others which lead off across the 'open fields' in every direction. The artificial tree lines clearly indicate that the town perhaps enjoyed a much richer display of vegetation than is the case today. The small plots behind the houses, often under an acre in size, are a pointer to the many other small holdings found in the larger fields beyond.

As Epworth has retained so many Victorian Buildings what we see on this old map is still very much a part of the local scene. Two of the old schools still remain, but in the Market Place the Red Lion Inn has lost its three companion inns, although the former Royal Oak building can still be seen. It is of interest to note the many water pumps and wells marked 'p' and 'w' respectively

Some of the larger rate payers were T.J.Blaydes with his factory in Chapel Street; James Hammond at his coach works in Queen Street and Thomas Thompson for his factory and mill. The amount paid by the Royal Oak Inn was 11s. 1d whilst the Rector, Canon Overton paid £2. 3s. 0d. The 1890 signatories were William P.Taylor and Henry Kelsey (Churchwardens) and George Walster and Charles Anderson - Overseers of the Poor. (REF.8)

The poor were still aided by the New Year's Day Clothing Charity - clothing tickets being distributed from a value of 2s. 6d. to 6s. 0d. each, and in 1879, these were given to 199 needy folk out of a population of 2178. Coals were also given to 79 people. In 1901 the poor rate had risen to 3s.0d. on buildings and 1s.0d on land and there was then a good deal of resistance to paying it.

In 1901 the population was 1856, of which 908 were males and 948 females, a total that then included railway construction employees who were residing temporarily at Epworth. The town had 479 inhabited homes and 480 families and the parish acreage of 6151 acres included land and inland water. We have noted some reasons for the population decline, but others were the fact that the recently increased railway facilities took stock away from a formerly important market; tradesmen from Doncaster and Gainsborough caused a decrease in profit of local trade and the number of people supported by town trade declined. (REF.9)

The Magistrate's Court in Hollingsworth Lane was erected in 1848. At one time the Chief Constable's house went with it, but when the Court was extended in 1983 his house was removed. Petty Sessions at Epworth were held every Thursday at the Police Station and there were many cases involving all kinds of strange misdemeanours. Many offences concerned misuse of the highway with horses and wagons, riding without reins being regularly cautioned. People were fined for not carrying a flag before a traction engine on a public road; keeping dogs without licences; failing to pay the poor rate; chicken stealing; trespassing, poaching or playing pitch and toss (*illegal gambling*); something I witnessed many times down the lanes around Hatfield in the 1940's.

There was an old Lock-up behind the Poor House in Queen Street, but it was pulled down to make room for a garden. It was a brick construction 8½ feet by 5½ feet with an arched roof 6 feet 8 inches from the floor to the top of the arch. The story goes that a prisoner once burrowed under the door to escape. Another lock-up was in the old cells which stood behind the three cottages standing to the right on entering Church Walk (REF.10)

# THE VICTORIAN SCENE

There was quite a concentration of industry around Epworth's centre in the middle years of the last century. George Batley was a currier and leather cutter in the yard between Solicitor's Terrace and the old printing works, and at one time this yard had seven one-up and one-down cottages situated there. The printing works itself (now a motorists' discount shop) used to be a chapel. There were more leather factories in High Street; tanyards and a malt kiln. The cottages opposite Harbour Light's Fish Shop were built for the malt kiln employees. Hammond Brothers, the coach builders in Queen Street, laid claim to have been the first Epworth firm to send goods abroad, their famous 'Ralli Cars' being exported to South Africa.

There were numerous shops and businesses, again mostly around the market place and adjacent streets. E.W.Atack was a grocer in the High Street and John Fox had a similar concern in West End Road. Mrs M. Gibson sold boots and shoes in the High Street and J.A.Brandish made them in his premises in Chapel Street. Other Chapel Street businesses were G.Newton, plumber and glazier and Alfred Bailey, ironmonger and agent for incandescent gas lights. Mr J. Bottomley' the town's famous photographer, who captured many wonderful scenes around the area (including the building of the railway), lived in the High Street and died on 11th November,1909 at the good old age of 80.

Mr A.E.Archer ran the Post Office which was also a pharmacy (then in Church Street) and he claimed *'guaranteed purity of every drug sold'*. Many businesses looked out on to the Market Place like Newbitts of London House, specialists in men's clothes; Shillito's hardware store where you could buy sacks, stack covers, rope, band and twine; Rimmingtons of Waterloo House in Hollingsworth Lane sold blankets, sheets and drapery and A. Travis made saddles and harnesses.

Emersons sold furniture as well as fruit and vegetables and had shops in both the Market Place and Chapel Street. S.Cooper was a tailor and general outfitter and there were many, many more shops and small businesses around the town then.(REF.11)

Time was when boring for coal was thought to be a good idea and it was tried at Lawns Farm which was situated out on the road to Belton. This boring found nothing at a depth of 43 yards, but at 91 yards a very thin seam was discovered. A coal pit was talked of as being a blessing to the town, but perhaps fortunately, talk was as far as it went !

The town authorities were not keen to have proper surface or underground drains either it seems, as in 1873 a Commercial traveller complained that soapsuds, sewage, foldyard muck and everything else liquid poured down through Epworth Market Place; flowed on down the High Street and formed a fearful cesspool by Dr. Pullen's house.

Epworth's Gas Works were erected in Tottermine Lane in 1864 at a cost of £2,000. The town lagged behind Crowle in obtaining gas lamps, making do with a few dim naphtha lights which were something of a joke in the community. A

Table Four

# LIST OF OCCUPATIONS FOUND IN EPWORTH IN THE 1850's

Auctioneers (3)
Baker / Flour dealer
Beerhouse Keepers (3)
Blacksmith (6)
Boot / Shoe Warehouse Keeper
Boot and Shoe Makers (12)
Bricklayers (4)
Brickmaker
Butchers (6)
Carriers (2)
Coal and Flour Dealer
Coal Merchant
Confectioner
Cooper (Barrel Maker)
Corn Millers (4)
Curriers (2) (Leather Dressers)
Drapers and Grocers (14)
Druggists (2)
Dyers (2)
Farm Owners (50)
Farmers (33)
Farrier
Fire and Life Office Agents (6)
Flax Dealers (15)

Flax Dresser
Flour Dealers (2)
Gardeners/ Seedsmen (3)
Glaziers (2)
Hairdressers (3)
Hatmaker
Horsebreaker
Ironmongers / Tinners (3)
Joiners (5)
Land Agent
Landlords of Inns (6)
Leather Cutters (2)
Linen Manufacturers (11)
Machine Owner
Malsters (2)
Manor Steward
Methodist Ministers (3)
Milliners (8)
Music Dealer
Omnibus Drivers (2)
Painter / Paperhanger
Parish Clerk
Photographer
Plumbers (2)

Postmaster
Potato Merchant
Printer
Printer / Publisher
Rector
Registrar
Rope / Twine Maker
Sacking Makers (3)
Saddlers (2)
Seed Merchants (2)
Shopkeepers (4)
Solicitors (3)
Stationers (2)
Straw Hat Makers (4)
Superintendent Constable
Surgeon
Surveyor
Tailors (8)
Tallow Chandler
Tanners (3)
Teachers (4)
Watchmakers (2)
Wine / Spirit Merchants (2)
Wheelwrights (6)

*Extracted from White's Lincolnshire Directory, 1856*

vestry meeting of September 1873, wanted to see gas lamps in Epworth placed in strategic positions and by the end of the 19th century, 54 were in use. The Gas Company received frequent complaints about the quality of the lighting and a remark at the Lighting Committee Meeting that the lamps were little better than half-penny candles was not untypical.(REF.12) The Epworth Gas Company, managed by the Thorpe Brothers in the middle of the present century, finally called it a day in February 1960, and contrary to some stories Horace Thorpe's wife, Violet, never actually shovelled any of the 13 tons of coal per day that the works consumed.

An excellent impression of the workaday life, and indeed the atmosphere of Victorian Epworth can well be imagined from a study of *Table 3* (extracted from White's Directory of 1856) which lists most of the various occupations found there in the 1850's. These have been placed in alphabetical order and the figures in brackets indicate the number of people or trades where they exceed one. Some people did two or even three different jobs and in the case of William Read (a jack of all trades), he is listed as being involved in printing, groceries, drapery, tallow, seeds, stationery, wines and spirits and publishing. The son of MrGeorge Ward, commenting in 1935, on his father's flax business, said that it was more profitable than ordinary farm work and it also provided winter work in the barns when there was little work outside.

Notice the large numbers in farming and its associated industries of flax dealing, wheel making and other concerns, and yet we see only one horsebreaker and no mole catcher. It is interesting to ask the question - how many of these businesses are still in town? Check them out and you will be surprised.

It is often said that folk had to make their own fun years ago and indeed they did. Amateur Dramatics were keenly executed; there was the brass band and the Band of Hope. The Mechanics' Institute Annual Soirees in the Temperance Hall were very popular. The Church had its Working Men's Society; there was a Town Debating Society and then all the various sports, tennis, football, cricket and hockey, and in general it seems that late Victorian Epworth was a popular and attractive little country town.

Let us leave the 19th century with a word about one of the town's institutions just briefly mentioned earlier, and I refer to the *'Epworth Bells'* weekly newspaper. These days we receive it on Fridays, but for many years it was published on Saturdays. Printed and published by Mr F. Barnes of Epworth it first came out as a single sheet, about the size of a hymnsheet, on Saturday 26th October, 1872. But for a short break of five months in early 1877, the *'Bells'*, as it is affectionately known, has appeared ever since. For years and years it cost a penny, but went up to three half pennies in 1942. Mr Samuel Breeze took over the paper in 1896 and it was in his family until 1981 when it passed into the management of the Lincolnshire Standard Group of newspapers. Its name may have originated from the use of Church bells or the sound of the bellman as he signalled some news, but this is only supposition. Foster Barnes loved poetry and the famous Tennyson quote, " *Ring out the old, Ring in the New; Ring out the false, Ring in the true,* " has featured in this much loved local paper since the 12th May, 1877.(REF.14)

REFERENCES
1. Information sheet. *A Summary of the History of Epworth Mechanics' Institute.*
2. Display Information about Epworth. The Epworth Society.
3. *Vestry Minutes. 1827 to 1843.* Lincolnshire Archives.
4. *Lincolnshire Notes and Queries.* Lincolnshire Archives.
5. *Epworth Town Trail.* (1984) op. cit.
6. *Epworth Bells Archive.* Mechanics' Institute Library, Epworth. 1872 to 1908.
7. *Epworth Town Trail* (1984) op.cit.
8. *Poor Law Rate Books. 1845 to 1890.* Lincolnshire Archives.
9. *Epworth Bells* Archive. (1872 to 1908) op.cit.
10. *Epworth Town Trail.* (1984) op.cit.
11. *Epworth Bells* Archive. (1872 to 1908) op. cit.
12. Ibid.
13. *White's Lincolnshire Directory.* 1858.
14. *Epworth Bells* Archive. (1872 to 1908) op.cit.

The Imperial Hall in Chapel Street dates from 1906 and has played an important role in Epworth's social life. It was a venue for Amateur Dramatics, films, dances, socials, concerts and public meetings. It still acts as Epworth's village hall and is used for a variety of purposes.

# CHAPTER TEN

## Right Up Your Street

Street names are often of interest, pointing the way as to how a town might have developed. Over the years some old road names have disappeared, but more and more new ones come along as required, sometimes causing disputes about their establishment. Of course many route titles are obvious enough, being named after their positions, particular people, or certain buildings. Here at Epworth, quite clearly, there was no Station Road prior to the coming of the railway, and in fact, nor was there any West End Road, for High Street used to run all the way out to what (as in hundreds of other places), was termed Town End.

The road leading westwards from Epworth is certainly one of the oldest roads, and entering the town along this route from Sandtoft we very quickly come to a selection of old and interesting buildings. Of particular interest are some of the former threshing barns which can be seen in several places, for example at No 58 and Home Farm in Station Road, and, standing back from the road, at Fieldhouse Farm. One at Selby Farm with cart-shed and stables (on the western edge of the parish) is being made into a private house. These old buildings are characterised by their large wagon entrance doors, breather slits and pitching hatches. The one alongside the road at No 58 Station Road is probably the oldest of these reminders of 'old time harvesting'. Its central bay is flanked by pilaster strips and it has a double board door beneath a timbered lintel. It has pitching hatches to the road and the gable ends and inside there is a three-bay collared rafter roof. Epworth is rich in Listed buildings and these old farm buildings are amongst many that will be considered in this section.

This area of the town has also some Listed stables, granaries and pigeoncotes to be seen at Poplars Farm and also in outbuildings belonging to Stockwith House. The three-storey building at Poplars Farm combines all three and has wrought iron figures on the gable-end showing '1808'. Tumbled brick to raised gables used to be a common feature and it can be clearly seen here. It will be noticed that the edges of the gable are finished with triangular wedges of brickwork to give a smooth finish to a straight gable without adding a stone coping. Such a style dates from around the 17th century and was in use in Lincolnshire and Yorkshire until well into the 19th century particularly in smaller houses and farm buildings.(REF.1) At Home Farm too is a further example of a pigeoncote with a stable and granary. The block is in yellow-brown brick with a pantiled roof. These buildings are probably contemporary with the threshing barn (to the north side of the courtyard) mentioned earlier. Once again we see the very common stone-coped gables with shaped kneelers. All the doorways here have large ashlar blocks for hinges and catches. Seeing these pigeoncotes makes one wonder whether at some earlier time pigeons may have been kept as a supplement to the

Threshing barn at 58 Station Road with its colour-wash hiding its red/brown brickwork. This building displays various styles of breathers and has three bays, the end ones having pitching hatches at first floor level. Inside it is typical of many such barns with its brick wall piers to the beams and the three bay collared rafter roof with pegged staggered butt purlins.

Former Tithe Barn at Poplar's Farm, West End Road.

***Old Threshing Barns in Station Road.***
Threshing barns are characterised by their pitching hatches; breather slits in various styles and their broad doorways. The above example is at Home Farm and dates from 1809.

This early 19th century threshing barn can be seen at Fieldhouse Farm - the site of John Harris's Haywain Farm Museum. Note the old advertisement on the foremost building which strangely enough is not a listed building. This view shows the north side of the barn and its south side edges the foldyard.

food supply. Of course Epworth has many examples of old granaries and the building which now serves as the refectory at Epworth's Old Rectory used to be a granary. It has been altered, but still has its granary loft and corbelled brick eaves, with a blocked attic hatch at the east end.

Grade 2 Listed buildings are also considered to have interiors worthy of preservation and Stockwith House (31 Station Road) has an original open-well staircase with a ramped and wreathed corniced handrail, column-on-vase balusters and newel posts with round knobs and profiled cheek pieces. This fine Georgian residence backs on to Home Farmhouse and at an earlier period all this block was just one house. It is fronted with twelve pane sash windows in flush wooden architraves and the addition to the north has a similar frontage. Many other old properties in Epworth have the fine open-well staircases inside and well known examples are The Old Rectory, Glen House, (24 High Street), Field House and Wesley Manse to name but a few. (REF.2)

It is natural that this part of Epworth should have been named West End Road, and then, after the coming of the railway, for the next section to be named Station Road. In regard to the more recently developed estates there has been a wish to probe back into history a little to find appropriate names for the new streets. In some cases ancient field names have been used as in the 'Vinegarth', 'Shepherds' Croft', 'Blow Row', and 'Eastfield Road'. (REF.3)

After mentioning the granaries it is natural that we should be drawn to the old mills that were once such prominent and workmanlike structures built on the higher ground around Epworth. It is believed that as many as six windmills once stood around the town, but these days just three remain to remind us of those busy corn-grinding days. A mill owned by a number of subscribers once stood back on the right hand side of the Belton Road, just past the mill which today is a private residence. It was believed that the Lord of the Manor could tax individual owners for the wind which blew over his land to drive the sails, but a subscription mill became popular being in multiple ownership and not therefore liable to this tax. The inscription which was on the side of this mill made its intention clear:

*'Both rich and poor a friend will find,*
*Who sendeth here their corn to grind.'* (REF.4)

This mill was pulled down in 1921.

White's Directory for 1896 names a William Storey as a miller, in addition to James Brooks, Richard Maw and Richard Thompson, names by which the present standing mills are known. Could it be that William Storey had some involvement with the subscription mill, although someone of the same name was also a farm owner at West Carr.

Maw's mill, currently under some restoration by a local enthusiast, stands on the rise to the north of Station Road, but is also very prominent from the Belton Road. Built of red brick, it consists of four storeys and in its heyday must have

*Above:* an early 19th century example of pigeoncote, granary and stable, all combined, and seen at Home Farm, Station Road.

*Left:* Another delightful range of the same sort of buildings, here seen at Poplar's Farm in West End Road.

Stable and granary at the Old Rectory. It was probably built some twenty years or more after the Wesleys left Epworth in 1736. Today it serves as a Refectory - a very acceptable amenity for the Rectory visitors.

Stockwith House, along with the present Home Farmhouse formerly consisted of one large family house. It displays a fine range of 12 pane sashes in flush wooden architraves.

*Left :* Maw's Mill dates from the late 18th century and is well positioned to have made the most of the varying winds in the days when its four sails were a prominent feature on the landscape.
*Right :* Thompson's Mill stands to the south, off Rectory Street and is one of only three tower mills in South Humberside which still retain most of their internal machinery.

An early view of *'The Gables'* at the corner of Belton Road and Tottermire Lane. It is a typical Victorian middle class family house and once belonged to the Tonge family, but is now used as Council Offices. *Courtsey of Miss Marjorie Trimingham.*

been a very impressive sight with its four enormous sails turning in the summer breezes. It had an iron wallower* with an integral ring underneath to drive the sackhoist. Its two-section upright wooden shaft drove the grinding stones on the second floor. It last saw service in the 1930's, but now appears a little forlorn in its isolated position overlooking the low land out to the west. The damaged fireplaces within, with their flues emerging as small vents at the second floor level, and the missing floors and roofing present a sad state of dereliction; yet there is still some dignity in this grand memorial to the miller's trade.(REF.5) A local resident has shown me copies of documents which refer to the building and pricing of this mill in 1783.(REF.6)

Brook's Mill on the Belton Road looks neat and tidy as a private house, and it too stands as an example of the four storey tower mill capped by a wooden cupola with a ball finish. Built about 1800 it was originally called 'White Mill', but was later tarred black, as were most tower mills. It was worked by wind power until the late 1940's, latterly with only two sails, and continued with engine power until 1960. Its machinery was removed in 1977 and is now at Skidby Mill, near Hull. The sails drove three pairs of grinding stones - two French and one Grey.(REF.7)

The third remaining example of a tower mill stands to the south of Rectory Street and it has been in the hands of the Thompson family for some 200 years. The ground floor has board doors to the north and south and single windows east and west; the first floor has four windows and the remaining upper floors each have windows to the north and south. All are beneath segmental arches and the windows have sandstone sills. It has a stepped and cogged brick eaves cornice and a low, 20th century roof. What is of great interest in this particular mill is the fact that it is one of only three in South Humberside which still retain most of their internal machinery.(REF.8)

The sails of this mill were blown away on the afternoon of Wednesday, 8th November, 1882 and like many other mills in the area it operated on just two sails for sometime. (REF.9) In their later years many mills were converted to steam, paraffin or diesel powered engines to drive their grinding wheels. The Second World War did Thompson's mill no favours, for a blast of a German flying bomb exploding some 200 yards away, twisted the headgear and made it unsafe. The remaining two sails and the dome were removed soon after hostilities ceased and so ended a long and illustrious record of grinding corn in this lovely old mill.

The oddly named Tottermire Lane branching away from the east end of Station Road might conjure up images of folk at one time staggering through a muddy morass in negotiating this thoroughfare, but such a conjecture would be way off the mark. The suggestion for the origin of this route is perhaps more fittingly explained by J.K.Johnstone where he tells us that 'teotha' was Anglo-Saxon for a

---

* Wheel at the head of the main vertical shaft.

Fieldhouse Farm on Station Road is an early 19th century residence showing a handsome doorcase with ribbed pilasters and reeded brackets carrying an open moulded pediment. The six-fielded panel door stands below a moulded lintel and radial fanlight in a round-headed panelled reveal.

'Little Shambles' at Epworth Turbary. In the late 18th century and early 19th century the commons where peat was extracted were divided into small plots and let for a very low rent. This old mid to late Victorian cottage is one of the least altered examples of a turbary farmhouse still surviving.

tithing and myre (maer) named the Anglo-Saxon boundary.(REF.10). Therefore to see Tottermire Lane as the boundary of the Epworth tithing seems quite in keeping with its position, which is still on the northern edge of the town. The Epworth Gas Company used to have their works in this lane and they supplied gas for street lighting and also entered into business selling gas appliances; something which was mentioned earlier when looking at Victorian Epworth.

Epworth's centre has numerous old houses and businesses, many of which are listed and which have seen as many as seven or eight generations come and go. The High Street in particular contains around half of the town's complement of Listed properties and there are numerous fine period constructions which are not included on the preservation list. The main street has the White Bear Inn, Wesley Memorial Church and its accompanying Manse, Schoolroom and caretaker's house, Kilham Memorial Church, twelve even numbered dwellings and just four odd numbered houses. All of these are considered to be worthy of particular importance and more than special interest in the lists drawn up by the Secretary of State for National Heritage.

The White Bear Inn has 18th century origins with later alterations, its gable bearing the date 1811 and its interior having a boxed-in spine beam and an inglenook fireplace. Kilham Manse (just across the road) is of red brick with ashlar dressings and today it serves as a popular residential home. The house dates from 1878 and was built by Henry Kelsey of Epworth at a cost of £700. We have commented on the architecture of the Welsey Memorial Church earlier on, but the style of all its surrounding buildings should be noted as being by the same architect, Charles Bell who ensured they were entirely in keeping with the appearance of the church. They help to form a most attractive completion of this unusually ornate and celebrated group of Methodists buildings.

Epworth has had its Post Office in various buildings over the years and earlier this century it stood in Church Street where it also served as a chemists and grocers under the management of Mr A.E. Archer. The present Post Office is one of the earliest surviving vernacular buildings in the Isle of Axholme for it represents (at least in part) an example of timber framing with mud and stud infill. It has pantile roofs throughout, a tumbled in brick to the raised gable and its three room main range was formerly four bays of timber framing. The Dutch gable to the street is of the mid 19th century and in general, for architectural enthusiasts, this house is worthy of attention both within and without.

Many of the High Street shops have retained the old wooden surrounds with their carved brackets and supporting moulded wooden cornices. Victorian features are prominent in ribbed pilasters, cornices and hoods, architraves, friezes and decorative brickwork. Examples of such can be seen in the construction of various shops between Kilham Memorial Church and the Market Place, mostly on the north side of the High Street.

In the Market Place stands the Manor Court on the site of an earlier building. In the 1850's it had an open ground-floor arcade with iron railings, but this was infilled later to give the present appearance. Fronted with fine red brick in Flemish bond, its five ashlar keyed and channelled elliptical arches on brick pilasters (with moulded ashlar bases and raised imposts) are a very prominent sight in the town centre. The rear coach-house with its double board doors was a later addition.

Balram's Restaurant, just off from the Market Place (number 27 Queen Street) is a Georgian family house dating from the early mid 18th century and is typical of many buildings of that period. Such large houses, former homes of the middle and upper classes can be seen again along the same street and also in Chapel Street. Similar to this Queen Street House is London House, on the other side of the Market Place, which has been a business centre in Epworth since Victorian times. Possibly older than many of the larger houses in this town, this house still has very early flush wooden architraves with sills beneath keyed cambered stucco arches. It stands next to the Red Lion Inn, a hostelry dating from the days of the Wesleys and still having its stable range and granary, the old coach entrance and many other interesting embellishments. One such is its stepped entrance with its wrought iron balustrade of plain rails with wreathed handrail. Common in many parts of Epworth we note once more the moulded eaves cornice and stone coped gables.

Passing on into Albion Hill (formerly called Lancaster Lane) buildings numbering four to ten comprise a continuous line of properties ranging in date from the mid 18th century to the mid late 19th century. A three storied residence, with shops, stands next to the very well known Albion House and both contain first floor window ranges of original sashes of twelve or sixteen panes. The shop front of Albion House has a panelled surround with ornate carved consoles carrying panelled dosserets, cornice and hood.

Continuing up Albion Hill (and noting the attractive 'Fern Villa' on the left) we pass round into Rectory Street. Just before doing so another example of the tumbled gable can be seen across in the entrance to Mowbray Street. The Old Rectory, John Wesley's home, is a Grade 1 listed building with red-brown brick in Flemish bond on its south front, which displays seven bays with the centre one slightly forward. The house has a double-spanned pantile roof, hipped to the west and gabled to the east. The western aspect to my mind, looked more attractive when it still had its extension. The former Rectory was destroyed by fire in 1709 and had it not been for the vigilance of the French maid on Sunday, 12th February, 1854, this house might well have suffered the same fate. On that date around 2.30pm, a fire broke out in the nursery and neighbours rallied round with a bucket chain and eventually doused the flames, for which the Rector (Rev Charles Dundas) was extremely grateful. Apart from its attractions as the Museum of the Wesley Home, the interior has many interesting points of

The inscription *above* was built into the wall of the old subscription mill situated on the eastern side of the Belton Road a short distance beyond Brook's Mill. Such a mill had a joint ownership with the interested parties. *Courtesy Edwin Harrison.*

The Epworth Gas Company's Victorian premises in Tottermine Lane. Their service was welcomed, but suffered many a complaint. The business closed in February 1960 when it had been ran by the Thorpe family for many years. *Courtesy of Miss Marjorie Trimingham.*

Epworth's Victorian Post Office pictured in Church Street around the turn of the century.
*Reproduced from 'Epworth and its Surroundings, 1903'.*

Later the post office was situated in the building on the left in High Street. It can also be seen that the *'Epworth Bells'* was then printed here. Today it is a newsagents.

The Manor Court House dating from 1803 replaced an earlier Court House which accommodated the Court of the Lord of the Manor of Epworth and Westwood. Today the ground floor houses the Drainage Board Offices and the Epworth Society's Information Centre, whilst the Mechanics' Institute Library is on the first floor.

This house in Queen Street dates from the mid-18th century and has a fine range of Georgian sashes. The chimney stacks have been added recently.

'London House'. Another very fine Georgian family house, later used for business purposes as we see today.

'Albion House', pictured centrally, one time residence of William Read who wrote the well known *History of Axholme* and was something of a Jack of all Trades.

Here we see Albion Hill before it was so named. It was then Lancaster Lane, seen here looking towards the Market Place. Note the water pump in the foreground.

*Reproduced from 'Epworth and its Surroundings, 1903'.*

construction, not least being the use of gypsum on its attic floor. The entrance hall has a restored basket-arched fireplace; old timber beams and framing are still there plus a collared rafter roof with pegged butt purlins.(REF.11)

In Rectory Street can be seen one of Epworth's restored Pinfolds, the other being in West End Road near the former Mission Church. Time was when these pounds were frequently in use as the Pinder went about his work of penning stray cattle in the Pinfolds at either end of town and only to release them on the payment of the subsequent fine. Many other streets and byways of Epworth will have their fascination and interesting facets of history and the writer hopes that this brief look at just some of them has whetted the appetite of the reader.

REFERENCES
1. Neave, David  *The Dutch Connection.* University of Hull, 1988.
2. Sites and Monuments Records. Numbers 10097/100, 10450 and 10455/6. Humberside Archaeology Unit. Isle of Axholme Survey, 1988.
3. Garner,Stephen.R. *Burnham. The Story of an Axholme Village.* Old Granary Publications, 1994.
4. *Epworth Town Trail* (1984) op.cit.
5. Dolman,Peter. *Lincolnshire Windmills,a Contemporary Survey.*1986.
6. Stafford,Jack  Personal Communication.
7. Dolman,Peter. (1986) op.cit.
8. Sites and Monuments Records. 7743 (1987) op. cit.
9. *Epworth Bells* Archive. (November 1882) op.cit.
10. Johnstone, J.K.  (1886) op.cit.
11. Sites and Monuments Records. Numbers 2451, 3783, 6394/5, 6530, 6532, 7743, 10096, 10434/5, 10437/49, 10451/4, (1986 to 1988) op.cit.

The present Post Office is housed in a 17th century building of great interest. It has some timber framing, mud and stud infill and examples of both tumbled and Dutch gables. Inside it has a 4-bay pegged collared rafter roof with arched collars. It is one of the earliest surviving vernacular buildings in the Isle of Axholme.

# CHAPTER ELEVEN

## Reflections on the 20th Century

H.R.Shipley, whose family lived at Scawcett Farm in the early years of this century (before emigrating to Canada) writes about Epworth in the early 20th century commenting, *"I can still recall the excitement of the drive through Epworth at night. When the glow of the shop windows intermingled with the light of the street lamps making eerie shadows across the road, the spirited animals would swerve one way and then the other, despite a tight rein. One of the spots which required some driving skill was around the market cross"*.(REF.1)

There have been many staggering changes since those nostalgic days in a century which has seen progress from horse-drawn transport to rapid jet plane travel across the world, not to mention the amazing sorties into space and on to the moon. Again, it would need a separate book to deal with the many changes that Epworth, like any other place, has experienced through these years. We delight in reminiscences of living memory and both Epworth's weekly papers, *The Epworth Bells* and *The Axholme Herald* often remind us of bygone days; the former in its *Milestones from the Past* and the latter in its Editor's ,*When I waz a Lad* series or Roland Whitehead's memories.

Who knows, somebody's wardrobe may still have clothing bought from London House before 1920 or a bit of hardware from Shillito's may still be about the backyard ! Edwardian Epworth had fewer inhabitants than today and naturally far fewer houses, The 1907, twenty five inch Ordnance Survey Map shows only one house beyond Fieldhouse out along the Burnham Road and no development at all to the south of High Street in what has now become Fieldside, School Close, Coronation Crescent, Stanfield Road and Morfield Grove. Similarly on Blow Row there was nothing to see until well into this century. The town still had the real old English agricultural feel about it; folk drew water from wells and street pumps plus there was the varied aroma of farmyards and pigsties pervading the atmosphere.

The farmers were still transporting their produce along roads that were better, but by no means perfect in places and as early as 1833 they had looked to the possibility of a railway through the Axholme area and their desire to see the *'Iron Horse'* roll through the Isle became more and more intense. A route crossing the Isle between Gainsborough and Selby was considered, but like many other ideas, nothing came of it.

George Hudson's proposal in 1846 for a line to join York to Gainsborough was rejected in the House of Lords. The Great Northern Railway's 1847 plan for an Isle route remained an idea and so did the following 1878 scheme of the Great Eastern Railway. So the agitation for a local line went on and on, in committee after committee and even the possibility of a tramway built along the existing

The Isle of Axholme Light Railway under construction at Blackbridge Cutting near Belton, which is now a picnic area.

*Courtesy Edwin Harrison*

The Epworth Station Road Bridge under construction with a contractors' locomotive down at road level on a portable track. The mainline will be on the embankment being built.

The *Epworth Bells* reported the following item on the 30th November, 1901, concerning the bridge being built as seen in the middle photograph.

### THE NEW RAILWAY AT EPWORTH, TREAT TO THE WORKMEN.

On Monday a very interesting ceremony took place at Epworth. The new line, which is proceeding rapidly has reached Epworth; about 400 people gathered to witness the first engine to cross the highway (Station Road). Attached to the engine was a wagon conveying members of the Light Railway Committee and friends. Cheers were given when the train crossed the road and at the cutting on the north side, three shots were fired showing the process of blasting the rock in the cutting.

roads was considered. However, with the passing of the Light Railway Act of 1898, real progress ensued and Board of Trade approval soon came for the laying of over twenty two miles of standard gauge track from Haxey to Reedness Junction.

The 20th July, 1899 was a red letter day in Epworth and the town was gay with bunting and banners for the occasion of the cutting of the first sod for the Isle of Axholme Light Railway. Across various parts of the highway large banners read *'Welcome'*, *'Long looked For'*, *'At Last'*, *'Patience Rewarded'*, *'Success to Agriculture'* and there were others. Miss Bletcher deftly turned the first sod with a silver spade before the official opening party trooped off to the Red Lion to suitably celebrate this wonderful event.

What a thrill it must have been for the crowd of around 400 people who waited at Epworth station site on the 25th November, 1901 to see the very first locomotive drawing an open carriage, cross the main road bridge to run on into the town's new wooden station. Work progressed until the whole stretch of line between Haxey Junction and Marshland Junction was completed. On the 2nd January, 1905, 325 tickets were sold, 200 of which were used by passengers from Epworth. (REF.2)

The Railway ushered in a new phase of life for Epworth for it bought visitors on excursions from many areas and in particular it carried in crowds wishing to see and learn about Epworth's Wesley connections. The line enabled local folk to get away to the East and West seaside resorts or even further afield. The earliest passenger timetables for this line show that Epworth had the benefit of three trains per day in the up and down directions. The 8.01am to Haxey enabled folk to get away to Lincoln or Doncaster and the 8.43 am northwards was useful for business in Goole and connections to Hull. A full history of this fascinating railway is being published in 1994/95 and will contain around 100 wonderful photographs and a comprehensive history therefore I propose not to delve into the line anymore within these pages.

The increasing number of cars combined with improved roads and more public transport systems saw the passenger element of this beloved little railway come to an end, when its last passenger train chugged along its romantic route on the 15th July, 1933 . Goods trains carried on for a further twenty years and more before the lines were lifted and stretches of the track became enjoyable strolls and nature reserves.

By now the town had grown accustomed to the Parish and Rural District Councils and the Vestry Meeting now largely concerned itself with Church affairs. With the coming of the First World War, Epworth's inhabitants, like folk throughout the Country, were asked to contribute to the National Relief Fund in support of the War effort. As much as eminent men tried to impress on Epworth's townsfolk the desperate need for financial support, that ever-present conservatism of the Isleonian did not totally accept the gravity of the situation and

## AXHOLME JOINT RAILWAY
(Third Class only.)

| | | WEEK DAYS | | | | | | WEEK DAYS | | |
|---|---|---|---|---|---|---|---|---|---|---|
| | | a.m. | a.m. | p.m. | | | | a.m. | p.m. | p.m. |
| GOOLE | dep | 7 18 | 11 50 | 5 30 | HAXEY JUNCTION | dep | 8 20 | 12 55 | 6 32 |
| Reedness Junction | arr | 7 31 | 12 3 | 5 43 | Haxey | " | 8 25 | 1 0 | 6 37 |
| Reedness Junction | dep | ... | 12 6 | 5 46 | EPWORTH | " | 8 34 | 1 9 | 6 46 |
| Eastoft | " | ... | 12 15 | 5 55 | Belton | " | 8 41 | 1 16 | 6 53 |
| Luddington | " | ... | 12 19 | 5 59 | CROWLE | {arr | 8 53 | 1 26 | 7 5 |
| FOCKERBY | arr | ... | 12 23 | 6 3 | | {dep | 8 54 | 1 29 | 7 6 |
| Reedness Junction | dep | 7 32 | 12 5 | 5 45 | Reedness Junction | arr | 9 2 | 1 37 | 7 14 |
| CROWLE | {arr | 7 40 | 12 13 | 5 53 | FOCKERBY | dep | 8 42 | 1 17 | 6 7 |
| | {dep | 7 41 | 12 14 | 5 54 | Luddington | " | 8 46 | 1 21 | 6 11 |
| Belton | " | 7 54 | 12 27 | 6 7 | Eastoft | " | 8 50 | 1 25 | 6 15 |
| EPWORTH | " | 8 1 | 12 34 | 6 14 | Reedness Junction | arr | 8 59 | 1 34 | 6 24 |
| Haxey | " | 8 10 | 12 43 | 6 23 | Reedness Junction | dep | 9 3 | 1 40 | 7 17 |
| HAXEY JUNCTION | arr | 8 14 | 12 47 | 6 27 | GOOLE | arr | 9 18 | 1 53 | 7 31 |

January, 1905.        Fares—Goole and Epworth (Third Class only), Single, 1s. 3d.; Return, 2s. 6d.

Reproduction of the first passenger timetable for The Axholme Joint Railway published in the Lancashire & Yorkshire Railway's booklet : *Epworth - What to see and how to get there, Jan. 1905.*

Epworth railway station looking towards the cutting north of the station. Note Maw's mill on the skyline (on the right) still with its sails. The station masters house (which still exists today) lies behind the wooden station buildings.

One of the many welcome banners that heralded the coming of the railway to Epworth, with the cutting of the first sod in 1899.              *Courtesy of Miss Marjorie Trimingham.*

a plan to have weekly house to house collections was abandoned and it was decided to have a single, once and for all, house to house collection.

Belgium had suffered severely as a result of German repression and the Women's Belgian Refugee and War Relief Association had a strong and active representation of ladies in Epworth who ensured that plenty of clothing parcels went off to the displaced persons as well as to the troops at the front.

It was not long before Kitchener's recruitment campaign reached Epworth in the form of a Sergeant who established his enlistment centre in the Imperial Hall. At a recruiting rally the Epworth folk were told that a tenth of Gainsborough's population had joined the colours and that Epworth had sent only eight men, when they ought to have sent eighty! More dignitaries pushed home the need to fight for the honour of the nation and when a chaplain, the Rev. Hankin Hardy appealed for recruits some twenty men stepped forward to join up. Five were from Belton, four from Althorpe, three from Owston Ferry, two from West Butterwick, one apiece from Graiselound and Crowle and the four remaining men were from Epworth being Charles Hill, Thomas Rimington, Arthur Coggan and Horace Fox. This was on the 29th October, 1914 and a short while later they were in action.

By January 1915 some of the Belgian refugees were living in Epworth and in the meantime the Volunteer Corps carried out rifle practice on the top of the biggest room in Mr Blaydes' factory and also their drill in the Imperial Hall. The 1914 Agricultural Show was badly affected by the War in regard to attendance and the takings, so it was decided to cancel the 1915 show.

More and more Epworth men went to the front line and sadly it was not long before news of fatalities reached the Isle and week after week the *Epworth Bells* featured reports of men being either wounded or killed. Possibly Epworth's first casualty was Private William Spencer of the 16th Battalion of the Canadian Scottish Regiment. He was the only son of Mrs Spencer of Albion Hill and had left Epworth some three years earlier when he had emigrated to Canada. He was killed in action in May, 1915 and in the same month Epworth's Turbary mourned the loss of Sergeant William Coggan at the age of 27.

Many of the letters in the *Epworth Bells* from men at the front give moving and vivid accounts of life in the trenches, and although it is clear that the men were trying to put a brave face on their experiences, the true horror of all that appalling carnage is all too evident. Some of them expressed their warm thanks for the parcels they received from the women of Epworth. Each of these parcels contained a shirt, woollen helmet, muffler, two pairs of gloves and a pair of mittens.

The Military Service Tribunal met frequently to consider applications for exemption from war service, most of which concerned people in agriculture and allied occupations. We read, *'An Epworth smallholder (39) seven acres, who said he had a wife and nine children under 17 years of age was (also) given*

The remains of the railway bridge on the road from Wroot to Epworth as it approaches Battle Green.

Looking in excellent condition for its close on a hundred years' standing, is the access tunnel behind Battle Green built under the Isle of Axholme Joint Railway. It was constructed to allow the farmers, Fields and the Browns to get to their fields.

*conditional exemption'*. Total exemption was not so common and most were allowed a very short time, as for example, *'The application of an Epworth farmer for the exemption of a labourer, aged 39, was unsuccessful, a month only being granted'*. Another case reads, *'The Rector of Epworth tried to get exemption for his gardener, aged 38, married with one child and large garden to do!'* He too was only given one month's exemption.

As the war progressed more of Epworth's families were to hear sad news of the loss of fathers and sons, the *Epworth Bells* of 6th January, 1917, signalling in a sombre new year in picturing no less than twelve men of Epworth killed as a result of the war. We can only surmise that the atmosphere of the town must have been heavy with grief throughout those four bitter years as news of more and more casualties was received in regard to the fine young men taken away on the grim battlefields of Northern France. There was a tremendous relief when at last this awful conflict came to an end.

Epworth's War Memorial was commemorated in the provision of the Thurlow Sports Field, although there can be no doubt (judging from correspondence in the *Epworth Bells* in the years after the war) that some people would have liked to have seen a more traditional cenotaph erected to remember the fallen. The plaque in the chancel of St Andrew's Church names 43 men who paid the supreme sacrifice and at the end of the south aisle a Roll of Honour remembers all of those who served in the Great War.

The town slowly recovered from the shock of the war and the Temperance Hall continued to serve as a cinema. The Epworth Amateurs staged a spectacular performance of 'Don Quixote' in April, 1923, when the picture of the cast included in the *Epworth Bells* was possibly the first illustration of that nature to feature in its post war pages.

People still walked long distances, but cycles were used more and more frequently and motor cars and lorries began to roll through the town in increasing numbers. The Fordson Ton Truck was selling at £220 and the farmers were replacing more ancient tractors with a new Fordson tractor at just £120! Street lighting had been limited during the war, but now there were regular meetings demanding an improved illumination. The Gas Company was rather slow in responding and in general the position was not very satisfactory. After the First World War, effort was made to improve the condition of Epworth's streets and approach roads and pavements were laid as more and more vehicles came on to the scene.

On Saturday 27th October, 1928, the very last of the two-horse drawn buses went off from Epworth to Doncaster, 'driven-off', it was said by 'petrol-propelled coaches of these modern days'. The horse drawn service had been in the Making family for over 50 years and in that time they had never missed a single Saturday journey to Doncaster; had made the trip 2,600 times and covered 83,000 miles.

Battle Green, pictured above in the early 1920's looking towards Station Road. The modern scene shown below shows but little change apart from the pavements and a better road surface.

*Top photograph courtesy of Miss Marjorie Trimingham.*

In the late 1920's and early 1930's it was natural that there should have been strong interest in the spread of electricity and a good piped water supply. Many of the surrounding areas were beginning to enjoy these facilities and the matter began to feature regularly at Epworth's Council Meetings. The efforts of the Gas Company to light up the streets were often criticised and Councillors looked with envy at places where electric power was installed. Pressure mounted and the 1930's proved a progressive decade in Axholme and from a situation where only Crowle and Epworth had electric street lamps, by 1938 most areas in the Isle were enjoying the privilege. This produced a brisk trade in electric cookers, irons, kettles, vacuum cleaners and other electrical devices.

Talking pictures arrived at the Imperial Hall, and Epworth obtained its real, proper picture house when the Rio (erected between Chapel Street and Queen Street) opened for business on 27th November,1938, showing its first film *'Rosalie'*, starring Nelson Eddy and Eleanor Powell. The site of the Rio had formerly housed a leather factory owned by T.J.Blaydes. The Rio was well patronised, especially by service personnel, but in 1970 it closed due to dwindling numbers. It re-opened in November 1971, managing to survive a further six years before finally closing in 1977.

Epworth's piped water supply was laid in the early 1930's; the price of a Fordson tractor had risen to £150 and twenty years after the end of the Great War, the Thurlow playing field (which had been purchased in 1920 to serve as Epworth's War Memorial) was formally opened in 1938 ! Epworth folk were again watching events unfold in Germany and 180 Air Raid Wardens were training in Axholme.(REF.4)

Epworth's new street lamps were extinguished as the Second World War hit the town curtailing sport, local drama and travel. Rationing came in with sweets and clothing coupons and people were encouraged to *'Dig for Victory'*. Paper, cardboard, silver paper and rose hips were all collected for the war effort and iron railings (no matter how decorative they looked before their finely appointed houses) were taken away to be melted down and transformed into armoury. In an upper room of the building on the corner of the Market Place and Hollingsworth Lane (later to serve as the National Westminster Bank) dances were held. We are told that such was the enthusiasm of these wartime dancers that the floor had to be supported by two specially installed pillars, which remain to this day.(REF.5)

Epworth was told to expect 372 evacuees from the bomb-shattered Hull, but in the event just under 200 arrived and were soon enjoying the novelty of real windmills, farm machinery and even poultry. A number of crippled evacuees were billeted in the Epworth Wesley Memorial and Kilham Memorial Church Schoolrooms for a time. Many local people will remember their wartime visitors with love and affection and in turn the evacuees themselves recall pleasant memories of their enforced, but very enjoyable taste of country life. Contact has

An interesting 'Then and Now' comparison as we look down High Street from its junction with Church Street to the traffic lights at the crossroads. *Above* we see the grocer, Robert Brown pictured with his horse outside his shop. There were no parking problems then, unlike the situation in the High Street today *(below)*. It is interesting to study the fronts of the houses and shops to note the changes, and 'Oh yes - that dog in the top photograph will make it safely across the road !'

*Top photograph courtesy of Miss Marjorie Trimingham.*

been maintained over the years and a happy reunion was held in Epworth quite recently.

Sad news came when the death of the first Epworth man to die in action in the Second World War was reported. It was Private John Kelsey, just 20 years old and he had been living with his grandmother in Battle Green. Six months later Private David Hill of High Street was also killed. Epworth sent out 126 men and women to serve in the three forces and they fought in places all over the world. With the end of the war the residents of West End Road held a tremendous VJ Day party on 8th September,1945 - a grand affair at which some 400 local residents sat down to a feast. The sad side of these celebrations was that the World War Two Memorial Plaque in St Andrews Church records the loss of seven men, residents of Epworth.

*The Epworth Bells*, which had began its illustrious career selling at a half-penny had risen to 2d in 1950 and in the same year the Epworth and District Agricultural Society held its 5th Annual Show. In that same year the Rio cinema was showing three different films a week and on the 6th to the 8th December, Epworth's Mowbray Players (with a cast of 19 local folk) presented *'Pride and Prejudice'* at the Imperial Hall. What sterling service that hall has rendered to the town with all the various events that have been staged there.

In 1953, Samuel Wesley's grave underwent yet another renovation and when the next one takes place, workmen will find a sealed jar containing details of the work carried out in August,1953. There was talk of the Old Rectory being sold off when a new vicarage was built; a proposition that upset a number of local people, but the situation was saved by the intervention of the Methodist minister, the Rev. John Goldsbrough, who was influential in persuading the World Methodist Church to purchase the building. It was bought by an interested donor for £4,500 and generously presented to the World Methodist Church. A short time later it was restored and prepared to serve as the Museum of Methodism that we see today.(REF.6)

Epworth's old Church and Board Schools had done the town proud, but with the coming of the new schools (mentioned earlier on) their achievements have passed into history, but the old buildings remain to stir the memory of many a resident as they recall the 'happiest days of their lives'. Both the old buildings are still in use; the Board School serving as an Inn and the former Church School providing a venue for various community events.

And so we come full circle to the growth of modern Epworth. Burnham Road saw its ribbon development and Blow Row was built up with its side estates. Tasteful infilling continues, but the old Market Place and town centre still retain a strong, ever abiding tie with the more leisurely times; days of perhaps a deeper and more satisfying contentment than we know today. Here still beats the very heart of the Isle of Axholme.

## REFERENCES

1. Shipley, H.R. — *The Lengthening Shadow.* Carillon Press, Canada. 1975
2. Oates, G. — *The Isle of Axholme Joint Railway.* Locomotive Paper No. 16. Oakwood Press, 1961.
3. *Epworth - What to see and How to get There.* Lancashire and Yorkshire Railway Publication, 1905.
4. *Epworth Bells Archive.* (1900 to 1938) op.cit.
5. *Epworth Town Trail.* (1988) op. cit.
6. *Epworth Bells Archive.* (1939 to 1945, 1950 and 1953/55) op. cit.

This photograph was taken to show the splendour of the Old Rectory's hipped roof. The attic of John Wesley's family home contains 'Old Jeffrey's Chamber', the nerve centre of the strange hauntings recorded in the Methodist Leader's famous Journal.